THE BUSINESS OF
INSURANCE

T0289684

THE BUSINESS OF INSURANCE

BY

A. J. WILSON

EDITOR OF THE "INVESTORS' REVIEW"
AND CITY EDITOR OF THE "DAILY CHRONICLE"

Routledge
Taylor & Francis Group

First published in 1904 by Methuen & Co. Ltd.

This edition first published in 2018 by Routledge
2 Park Square, Milton Park, Abingdon, Oxon, OX14 4RN
and by Routledge
711 Third Avenue, New York, NY 10017

Routledge is an imprint of the Taylor & Francis Group, an informa business

© 1904 Taylor & Francis

Publisher's Note
The publisher has gone to great lengths to ensure the quality of this reprint but points out that some imperfections in the original copies may be apparent.

Disclaimer
The publisher has made every effort to trace copyright holders and welcomes correspondence from those they have been unable to contact.
A Library of Congress record exists under ISBN

ISBN 13: 978-1-138-55490-0 (hbk)
ISBN 13: 978-1-138-56742-9 (pbk)
ISBN 13: 978-1-315-12426-1 (ebk)

THE BUSINESS OF
INSURANCE

BOOKS ON BUSINESS

Crown 8vo. 2s. 6d. net.

Other volumes will be announced later.

THE BUSINESS OF INSURANCE

BY

A. J. WILSON

EDITOR OF THE "INVESTORS' REVIEW"
AND CITY EDITOR OF THE "DAILY CHRONICLE"

METHUEN & CO.
36 ESSEX STREET W.C.
LONDON
1904

PREFACE

THIS little book is in no sense intended to be of use to insurance experts. It is written by an outsider mainly for the ignorant, for the multitude who either wish to insure their lives, or to whom the insurance agent is for ever coming with his proposals, his promises and blandishments. My doctrine is that every man ought to insure his life the moment he arrives at a period or a position when his responsibility extends over the lives of others. If this duty were regarded as an imperative one by the community at large, there would be little or no necessity for the elaborate machinery required by our life offices to induce people to invest in life or other insurance policies; but as long as apathy prevails, such agencies must be maintained and a ceaseless activity displayed by the offices in tempting investors to enter into policy contracts. I write

to help the tempted. That is the one purpose
of this little book, and the various excursions
into other branches of insurance business than
life insurance in its various forms are only intended to convey a little superficial instruction
in as light and untechnical a style as possible,
so as to encourage readers to master the one
definite piece of teaching the book contains. I
trust it will serve its purpose, and help many
people to a right understanding on a matter of
such vital importance to their peace of mind and
to those who come after them. The pitfalls of
life insurance in these days are numberless, but
it will be easy to escape most of them, if not all
of them, by acting as here directed.

CONTENTS

vii

CHAPTER VI

CHAPTER VII

CHAPTER VIII

THE
BUSINESS OF INSURANCE

CHAPTER I

GENERAL NOTES ON LIFE INSURANCE

FEW modern institutions touch the daily life of communities more intimately than life insurance. It is essentially a product of modern civilisation, and implies two essential qualifications for success. The first is continuous peace, and the second is continuing debt. Life insurance is thus the outcome of a high state of civilisation as now understood. We cannot imagine a business of this kind existing and really flourishing in Great Britain during the long struggles between England and France, during the Wars of the Roses, or at the time of the Puritan conflict with Charles I. Down to the Revolution of 1688 we may say that this country afforded no scope for

B

the development of a business of this description,
and if that was the case with England, how much
more so with continental nations, always at war
with each other, subject to continual social dis-
turbances—not merely through disputes about religion and civil liberty, such as lay at the root of
the later civil conflicts in England, or to dynastic
conflicts, but to the aggressive spirit developed
among the democracy, now in one section of the
continent, now in another? No one could imagine
the Italy of the Middle Ages as a field for the
development of life insurance, and were the now
ancient and apparently solidly established civilisa-
tions of Europe again to become unstable, and
conflicts to break out, one of the first of their
products to suffer, and perhaps to disappear, might
be life insurance.

But peace within is only one of the essentials to
the successful pursuit of this form of insurance
business. Life insurance especially implies also a
revenue from interest, and interest is a product
which postulates debt. Debt also cannot come
into being in any fashion to be depended upon
except when order is completely established within
the state, when everything is submissive to established laws and customs. Without that essential

qualification nothing is secure, not even mortgages on private property, still less the rent paid for the usufruct of such property, or bonds upon the public revenue.

What then is this business which demands such breadth of foundation? Is it something akin to that " mutual aid " amongst animals and mankind, about which Prince Kropotkin has written so interestingly in a recent book of his bearing this title? In some of its aspects it is just that, but a form of " mutual aid " altogether different from what Kropotkin is dealing with; not different in spirit, perhaps, but essentially of an artificial instead of a natural or (shall I say?) humanitarian character. The first beginnings of life insurance in this country were extremely feeble, and do not yet date back three centuries. It is, indeed, recorded that an office of insurance within the Royal Exchange in London granted policies of life insurance of some sort in the end of the sixteenth century, and there is a case recorded of a dispute in the law courts over one of its policies, but the policy was not at all of the same description as those with which modern and genuine life insurance has made us familiar. It was simply a bet on the life of a man for one year entered into for the benefit of a third party. The office or association that took the money undertook to pay this third party £383 6s. 8d. provided the individual on whose life the policy was effected by him died within twelve months, and the rate of premium charged was 8 per cent. The policy seems to have been underwritten precisely in the same fashion as marine insurance policies are dealt with at Lloyd's, and were probably then dealt with.

Our oldest life-insuring offices, however, are the Royal Exchange Assurance Corporation and the London Assurance Corporation, both of which came into existence in 1720, when the South Sea Bubble burst. They began to issue life policies in the year following their incorporation, and are in existence to this day, strong and prosperous, if not of the magnitude of some of their younger competitors. There seems, indeed, to have been an older office called the Amicable, chartered by Queen Anne in 1706. Its business has long been merged in that of the Hand-in-Hand Office, but we do not gather that it did much, if any, life business, and the Hand-in-Hand certainly did not take up that line until 1836. Among the old offices our most conspicuous is the Equitable, which

came into existence in 1762 as a purely mutual
life office, and so successfully has its business been
conducted that it remains to this day one of the
most prosperous of our life insurance societies,
carefully and economically managed, rich and
select.

But in what does the business conducted by
these life insurance companies consist? In one
sense it is a betting business. It takes hazards
against death, seemingly reckless hazards from
one point of view. A young man for example,
at the age of twenty-one, desires to insure the
payment of £100 to his relatives in the event
of his death. In order to do this he undertakes
to pay so much per annum, either during the
whole of his life or for a fixed period of years.
The payment is, compared with the apparent
risk, in all cases at first sight ridiculously small.
In the case of some of the best offices it may be
less than £2 per annum. Should the purchaser
of this contract die within the first year, the £100
he has bargained for is paid over to his heirs.
Surely this looks a touch-and-go sort of business,
but it is not really so, for reasons which I shall
proceed to furnish.

Were two or three people to enter mutually

into this kind of contract, one with the other, the risk of loss to survivors would be too great to be borne ; but the secret of the ability of life insurance offices to enter into such bargains lies in the averages upon which they work.

For a long time after mutual offices and joint-stock companies began to conduct this description of wagering against death, they worked very much in the dark. In its earlier years, I believe, the Equitable Life Office charged 5 per cent. premium upon the amount insured, no matter what the age of the policy-buyer might be, and it was not until many years had elapsed that the business began to be systematised and its true risks established with scientific exactitude. As late as 1771 the Equitable Life Office charged a premium of £4 1s. 5½d. per annum for insuring £100 upon the life of a person aged thirty. At the present day a non-participating life policy can be procured from the same office by a person of this age for a premium of £2 0s. 1d. per annum. Other offices make the bargain come cheaper, in appearance at least.

One thing that almost compelled the pioneers in life insurance business to charge high premiums was the complete ignorance existing with regard to the average duration of life at different ages, or indeed at any age. They worked completely in the dark as to the nature of their risks, and had to guard themselves against loss by charging high premiums. Gradually, however, this ignorance was dispelled, but for many a year—one might say until well into the nineteenth century, when the Institute of Actuaries was formed and set to work to accumulate data in order to establish a scientific basis for the business—the offices had only such imperfect guides as the Carlisle and Northampton tables of mortality provided them with—tables compiled from the death statistics of these two towns, statistics naturally imperfect because deduced from the experiences of longevity in a limited population. Now, however, the average duration of human life, taken at every age from birth to a hundred years, has been established by the accumulation of an enormous mass of authentic statistics; and so exact are the results now tabulated that every life office is in a position to tell almost to a penny the extent of its risks upon each contract entered into. Hence in part the reduction in the scale of premiums, hence also the difference between premiums that insure merely the sum named in the policy and premiums entitling owners of the policy to a share in what are called the " profits."

Having ascertained the nature and limits of the risk of mortality, what is the principle on which these institutions guide their business, found their contracts? It is the principle of compound interest. Having ascertained the exact amount necessary to levy upon policy-holders in order to secure the offices selling the policy against loss on the average of all the lives insured, the next thing to settle, so as to reach the exact sum safely promisable, is the rate of compound interest at which the net premiums as received and invested may be expected to accumulate. Supposing, to reverse the process, a young man becomes possessed of £100 at the age of twenty-one, and invests this in a security bearing 5 per cent. interest, how long will it take this £100 to become £200, provided the interest received each year is forthwith reinvested at the same rate? That is to say, the first year's interest of £5 is placed in the same security, and in the second year that £5 also adds 5s. to the amount received on the total invested, and so on until the £200 is reached. How long time must elapse before the original capital is in this way doubled? On a 5 per cent. basis, rather less than fifteen years. Suppose, on the other hand, that the rate of interest is only 2½ per cent., it will take nearly twenty-nine years to make the £100 £200.

These examples should enable the reader to grasp the underlying principles upon which insurance offices conduct their business. It would, as a rule, be useless for two or three people to club their life premiums together and invest them in this fashion, and not very profitable, perhaps, for merely several hundreds to do so ; but an office which has so established its business that it is able to command an income of many thousands per annum, drawn from the large body of people, the thousands who have entered into contracts with it, is able to place this money out to advantage when the country in which it conducts its business is settled, when the wealth-producing or utilising activity of its civic, mercantile, or national life leads to the creation of many forms of debt of a more or less enduring kind, and when each year's premiums as invested accumulate at compound interest. The office is then in a position to do exactly for the individual Englishman what he himself might do if he had at the beginning so much capital to put aside and leave undisturbed for accumulation in exactly the same fashion. Its conductors know within very narrow limits what the claims upon the office will come to in an average of years upon a given volume of business, how much they can lay by permanently, what the rate of accumulation at compound interest will be, and how much, therefore, they can afford to promise the insurant, exact allowance made for the ascertained average risk of death.

Remarks of this kind may read dryly enough, but the dryness must be borne with, and the rudimentary elements of the business mastered before much progress can be made in enabling the public to arrive at some conception of the character and limitations of this most modern form of mutual aid—highly scientific, if you will, but also perfectly artificial. One may say that without our National Debt it would never have been possible for life insurance business in this country to develop and attain anything like the proportions it now exhibits. We were the pioneers of life insurance amongst modern nations, it may be added, because we were the pioneers of national debts. Down to a period long posterior to the Revolution of 1789, France had no well-secured debt. The king of the old régime had debts,

both private and state, but they were created by
each monarch on his own initiative, or arose from
the necessities of his absolute administration, and
offered no national security akin to that with
which our debt, the product of parliamentary
vote and sanction, was from the first endowed.
Kingly bankruptcies were by no means infrequent.

Without well-secured debts, the interest upon
which can be relied upon as absolutely as the
successions of seasons, life insurance business could
not exist in any satisfactory manner. Precarious-
ness in the receipt of interest upon money invested
would necessitate extraordinary precautions on the
part of offices granting life policies. The business
would, if it existed at all, soon degenerate into a
more or less rank gamble. Calculations as to the
speed at which money coming in would accumulate at compound interest would be continually
upset, and every now and again a wave of insolvency might sweep over the state or community
that might bring life and most other forms of
insurance business to a standstill.

Mention of the necessity for stability in the rates
of interest naturally leads me to discuss other
aspects of this investment side of life office
business. It had long ago passed beyond a state

of dependence upon merely national debts. At the present time the life companies existing in this country have accumulated resources to the amount of nearly £260,000,000. This feat would have been impossible but for the multiplication of public securities into which the money could be transferred. Were a time to come when no more securities could be created, whether through the impossibility of loading a nation with further debts, or through exhaustion in other directions, limits would be placed upon the capacity of life offices to issue policies. The limits would be of various descriptions. Assuming everything else to remain unchanged and the volume of securities to be no longer capable of increase, then competition for these securities would reduce the rates of interest obtainable upon invested money, and life offices would be compelled at once to reduce correspondingly their tempting offers to those desirous of taking out policies. We saw this law in operation to a limited extent while the sinking funds in Consols, established by Mr. Gladstone and other Chancellors of the Exchequer, were in full operation, that is to say, down to 1896. These sinking funds absorbed each succeeding year an additional amount of the capital of the National

Debt. So much debt was each year bought in and, to the extent of the amount of the sinking fund, cancelled, and the said amount automatically expended as the interest upon each year's redeemed stock became available for buying in more stock. As a consequence, the supply of this particular security diminished and its price advanced until it was no longer profitable for our life offices to place any more of their money therein. Most of them realised either all or the greater part of their Consols at the high prices and thus made handsome profits upon their capital, which could be invested to greater advantage elsewhere. Not one of them could afford to buy a stock at a price which yielded little more than 2 per cent. The money thus released found, however, other securities in which it might be placed at figures which still yielded a rate of interest as high as, and probably higher than, that upon which the more careful offices based their expectation of accumulations at compound interest. This perhaps seems abstruse, but I will try to explain it all later if the reader will bear with me meanwhile.

Changes of this description constantly going on involve changes in investment, risks of an unforeseeable kind, and the past generation has witnessed an enormous and continual variation in the position of all life offices in this respect. They have been impelled by the scarcity and dearness of the highest class of investments to spread their money over a variety of interest-bearing securities such as did not exist, and would not have been thought of a generation ago as offering the requisite degree of safety. No full details are given with regard to their investments, but whereas fifty or sixty years ago the life offices had no important outlets for their moneys beyond British Government stocks and mortgages upon real estate throughout the United Kingdom, you cannot now pick up any life insurance office's report without finding large sums invested in Colonial or Foreign Government securities, in Colonial or Foreign Municipal securities, in Colonial and Foreign Railway debentures, in Indian Railway stocks, in mortgages outside the United Kingdom, and occasionally in unsecured or badly secured debentures of trading corporations, or even in the unsecured stocks of Home and Foreign Railways. What do I mean by "unsecured"? In this instance I mean ordinary stocks with no capital below them, between them and loss through a falling off in revenue.

These changes imply considerably increased risk of loss, and that also is a limitation to the indefinite extension of this kind of business. To be safe it ought not to run any risk of loss of capital, but directly money is invested in any form, risk of loss of capital is implied. Indeed, were there no risk of any description, one might say that in most cases there would be no interest earned. The risk, however, is unquestionably augmented the further afield investments are carried, and in our day it has become more and more a source of anxiety, to life offices especially and to all bodies entrusted in a fiduciary capacity with large sums of money. They must, as the masses of this money become greater, run greater risks, because the proportion of risk to the amount of the capital invested tends to grow larger as the capital sunk accumulates. All the life companies can do is to spread these risks as widely as possible, and to try to select the best amongst the multitudes of investments offering. Mistakes of judgment might involve heavy losses, and even the most careful selection and unremitting vigilance cannot prevent unforeseen influences from coming into play to bring about loss when least expected. The recent story of our National Debt and our Municipal and Railway debenture and preference securities illustrates how danger may arise. Thanks mainly to the enormous cost of the South African War, and likewise, in part, to the consequent complete cessation of purchases for the National Debt sinking fund, as well as to the rapid multiplication of securities of this class, prices for securities esteemed of the highest class have declined by 10 to 15 and even 20 per cent. compared with what they stood at five years ago. Shrinkages of this kind could not be foreseen, and all that is left for institutions caught by this backward wave is to provide for the losses out of their accumulations. If they can do all this without in any way breaking their promises to their clients, they are fortunate.

CHAPTER II

SOME VARIETIES OF LIFE INSURANCE

LIFE insurance takes many shapes in these modern days. Thanks in no small degree to the strenuous competition of offices from the other side of the Atlantic, British life offices have been compelled to move forward out of the old rut of whole life policies, with or without a share in the profits, and to endeavour to tempt clients with alluring projects in bewildering variety. One of the now favourite methods of enticing the Englishman to insure his life is what is called an "endowment" policy. Instead of paying a premium during the whole course of one's life, a term of years is selected—it may be ten, it may be twenty, or any other number—and the individual who takes the policy is called upon to pay a premium only for that selected period. At the end of it he is generally presented with several alternatives.

Either he may take the sum contracted for in cash, or he may allow the policy to lie and profits upon it to accumulate, the whole to be paid to his heirs after death, or, still further, he may elect to take an annuity representing either the whole capital value of the policy or some portion thereof, representing, say, the interest upon the accumulated profits, leaving the original sum assured to be paid to heirs in the usual manner.

Policies of this description have become remarkably popular of late years, and in some respects deservedly so. The great temptation they offer is that an insured person is relieved of the burden of premiums in the later years of his life, when, it may be, he has less available means. The offer of an annuity at a given date, moreover, presents a great attraction, as likewise the prospect of receiving a sum down, which might be invested in any way the recipient pleases. The character of life insurance, however, has been greatly altered by this endowment system. It has become a much more selfish affair than it originally was. An insurant now saves for himself, not for his offspring. Also a speculative element has been brought into the business of a sort which did not formerly prevail there to anything like the same extent. Men are tempted to over-insure in the hope that they may be able to continue for a term of years to pay excessive premiums, so as by pinching and self-denial to secure a large sum of money at the end of the period. Often the consequences of this is disaster in the shape of abandoned policies and lost premiums. This is especially frequent when the offices taking the contracts are low-grade and unscrupulous. The system also opens the way to all manner of more or less delusive prospects of gain, and in dressing these up for the beguilement of a public innocent of any knowledge of figures the American life offices stand pre-eminent. I have an old quarrel with them on this and other accounts which I am not going to open up here, especially as some English offices have taken to imitate to a needless extent American methods, with the result that their working expenses have risen beyond all fair and honourable proportion to the requirement of the business and the interests of their clients ; but I must be allowed to express regret that a change of this kind should have gone so far and been allowed to taint so deeply the straightforward, economical, and prudent habits of business with which our leading English and Scottish life offices have long made us familiar.

A class of office that ought to be avoided, no matter how tempting the offers may look, is the " assessment," " natural premium," or " fraternity " class. They are all at best pure delusions. For a time offices of this description had considerable vogue in the United States, and every one of them in a more or less brief period came to grief. A recent report of the Insurance Commissioner of the Commonwealth of Massachusetts gives some particulars regarding about a score of these offices in process of winding up. In every instance the result for the clients is disastrous, and it cannot be otherwise. Unfortunately the mistaken—zeal, shall I call it?—of American insurance reformers led to the importation of this " assessment " system into the United Kingdom, and the fruits here likewise have been, or promise to be, nothing short of disastrous. Yet the statements put forth by these sham life offices are often of a quite plausible description, when we consider the fatal ignorance of the general public in regard to everything relating to life insurance. A pretence is put forward that reserves are unnecessary if there be true mutuality, and the prudent accumulations of well-established life offices are seized upon as an argument in favour of what is called the " mutual reserve" or "fraternity" or "natural premium" system.

Ordinary life office reserves are treated as if they represented a robbery of the public, and it is contended that if premiums were confined to small sums to cover working expenses and some small unforeseen contingencies, the true way to meet claims is to assess the members of the "mutual" company or association each month, or quarter, or fixed period of some kind, for the exact amount of the claims that have meantime fallen in. The practical outcome of this method of conducting business is that after a few years these assessments invariably become intolerable to the policy-holders, many of whom consequently drop out, receiving nothing whatever in exchange for the sacrifices they have made. Their contract is broken, and there are no funds in hand out of which to give them compensation in the shape of surrender value or anything else. The low premiums asked at entry and during the first year or two are therefore merely in the nature of bait for gudgeons, and the expenses of such companies or associations are always on such an extravagant scale that they very soon disappear in bankruptcy. Those that struggle on do so at the expense of their clients, and without conferring a substantial benefit upon anybody outside the small number of people interested in keeping the thing going for the sake of what they can make out of it.

Insurance of this description is root and branch dishonest, and the public cannot be too strenuously warned against having anything to do with it. Choose instead companies or mutual offices that have accumulated large reserves. It may be that in most cases these reserves represent to a small extent restricted or even niggardly distribution of profit or bonuses on policies that in the past have become claims, but it is much better for the intending insurant that an office should thus have in its possession excessive reserves against unforeseen risks and uncalculated-on losses, than that there should not be enough money in hand to go round.

Mention may be made here of the Albert and European Life Offices, which came to grief in 1869. Neither of these offices would have stopped payment if it had accumulated large reserves. At the date of its suspension the Albert Insurance Company, whose contingent liabilities were at least £3,250,000, had funds in hand to the amount of only £271,500. The European Assurance Company, again, whose liabilities on policies ran into many millions, had less than £500,000 in hand as life assurance fund. The consequence was bankruptcy and enormous losses to both shareholders and policy-holders, losses against which both would have been protected had the businesses been conducted on honest lines. The immediate cause, however, of the failure of both these companies was the criminal extravagance they had indulged in as absorbers of other life offices. Within comparatively a few years the Albert Office had bought up some twenty-one different agencies or companies, and had paid no less than £238,000 for the goodwill of such. Most of these acquisitions had only been in existence a few years, and, as the *Economist* pointed out at the time, almost any life insurance corporation can show good figures for the first two or three years of its existence. The policy-holders it rakes in do not begin to die until some little time after they have become members, and consequently to buy up such raw ventures, giving more or less excessive sums for their "goodwill," was the surest possible way to lay the foundations of swift disaster. As a measure of the extravagance which led to the catastrophe of 1869, it may be mentioned that the board of the Albert Company paid £100,000 for the business of a company called the Bank of London and National Provident Life Association, which had only been seven years in existence. For another concern called the National Guardian, whose age was six years, it gave about £17,000, and so on. Not only was this money wasted, but the company assumed liabilities on policies in a reckless fashion, which speedily brought it to the ground.

Are there any offices in a similarly rotten state to-day? Such a question cannot be answered offhand, but I do not know of the existence of any British office whose business is in a position at all comparable with that of the Albert and European Companies at the date of their suspension. That suspension, indeed, was of incalculable benefit to the general body of life-policy holders in this country. It stirred up the good offices to reform some of their methods of administration, to vigilance in the selection and supervision of their investments, and in many other ways did much good. If we have the seeds of trouble amongst life offices to-day, they will lie in other soil. They will spring from such causes as the failure of large and important classes of their investments, or from the calculation of the rates at which money is expected to accumulate on too high a scale.

Most British companies of the old-fashioned type must be considered as near absolute safety as anything human can be. There are, however, a few native companies which conduct business upon an extravagant scale, which assume risks which their neighbours look upon as dangerous, which, for instance, conduct extensive business abroad in life insurance policies under conditions that do not always or often make for profit. It will be well, therefore, to avoid such offices, and it can very easily be done by applying to all the ratio of expenditure to premium income test, to be described later.

Some of our life offices in recent years have taken risks on life policies without a previous medical examination of intending insurants. Most of the companies, however, still adhere to the old fashion of compelling the candidate for a policy to pass a medical examination before acceptance, and some of them still utilise any doubtful item in a medical report as an excuse for adding to the premium. Suppose a young man of twenty-five desires to take out a policy of £500 in one of these offices, and that in the medical examination, or in the paper of questions he answers, mention is made of some relative, it may be a distant relative, who has died of a transmittible disease ; the excuse is still often seized upon to refuse to accept this life except by adding so many years, so that the policy is granted as at the age of thirty, or it may be thirty-five. This fashion used to be quite prevalent, and there was a good deal of dishonesty to be found in carrying on business in such a style. Competition, however, has pretty well eliminated this element of extortion from the practices of the most reputable life offices, so much so that I am disposed to say to anyone who is met by a device of this sort, the best thing he can do is to decline to take out the policy and apply elsewhere.

When an office steps outside the candidate's own state of health and rakes in contingent possible risks, it is better to withdraw at once. I know an instance of a man now well over sixty years of age who, on taking out as a youth his first policy, was compelled to pay the scale of premium on a life ten years older than he was because some distant relation had died of consumption, his own health being perfect. Such a payment meant a heavy annual robbery, and the robbery was emphasised some dozen years later by the same office taking the same life as first class on another policy. I prefer to this kind of thing the offices that accept lives without any medical examination whatever. The risks they run by so doing are not so very great. If the business is large, the average of the claims arising will not be appreciably higher than where the medical examination has to be undergone as a preliminary, and an office can always protect itself, to some extent at least, by postponing for a few years the date at which it will recognise the policy as valid for a claim to be paid in full.

Besides these forms of insurance—or insurance so called—I must notice a branch of the business which has grown up within the present generation and assumed enormous proportions. This is called "industrial" insurance. The name is a misnomer, for it is really "burial money" insurance, and consists in the sale of policies for definite sums to the working classes, the poor, in exchange for premiums collected in pennies, twopences, and sixpences per week out of the weekly wages of those who buy these policies. Business of this sort has apparently proved to be an irresistible attraction to multitudes amongst the working classes, and has given rise to not a few scandals, especially where infant lives have been insured. Children, and even aged persons, have often been made away with in order that the burial money, or "industrial" policy, be it only for a five-pound note, may be secured by those who have paid the pence. Of late years this shady side of the business has been less prominent, and I trust, though I am by no means sure, its gradual disappearance indicates an advance in the moral sense of the community. In other respects, however, industrial business is anything but free from objectionable features. One of the most prominent of these is the necessarily high ratio of working expenses. Even the best-managed offices spend in expenses and commissions about eight shillings out of every pound paid in by their policy-holders. It follows that the burial money is bought at a very high price by the people who in this way insure. In spite, however, of this excessive-looking rate of expenditure, the business has proved to be remarkably profitable, so much so that I know more than one instance of companies organised to conduct this class of business that have been able to lift themselves out of a

position of insolvency into one of prosperity,
merely by help of the enormous gains accruing
through the collection of these weekly coppers.
They trade upon the complete ignorance of their
victims by giving them much less for their money
than they could afford to do, and by making the
low sum originally granted the maximum of the
policy, no matter though the premium payments
exceed it twice over, apart altogether from investment accretions.

To working men or women the offer of £6 or
£8 or £10 at death in exchange for a weekly payment of a few pence seems generous. They are
unable to understand that the accumulation at
compound interest of even half the money continually paid in by them may come to represent
in many cases more than twice the amount of
their policy, and are therefore an easy prey to the
energetic and unscrupulous canvasser. All the
money over after meeting claims becomes the
property of the individuals who have formed
themselves into a company to carry on this business. There is no liability beyond the amount of
the sums insured, and after a few years the interest
income on accumulated funds may be merely an
addition to the profits of the business. A great

reform is wanted in this branch of life insurance, if it deserves such a name.

Many years ago I advocated the intervention of the Post Office in conjunction with the Friendly Societies as a means of counter-working these industrial insurance companies, and of securing fair play for the poor. Nothing came of the recommendation, which was founded on an extensive study of the reports and evidence published by the Royal Commission on Friendly Societies, and I am not sure now that I should put forward the same views. Our Post Office, like other Government departments, is, on the average, so indifferently managed, so liable to be encrusted over with abuses, and so completely a victim of routine, that I doubt whether an efficient system of industrial insurance could be entrusted to its management. Moreover, some of the offices doing this class of business already in the field have become so powerful, particularly one or two of them, within the present generation, that it would be next to impossible to dislodge them from their almost impregnable position. The only thing we can hope for is that the richest of these offices will improve their methods of treating the people who come to them with their weekly pence, by giving them either larger fixed sums in exchange for these pence, or by cutting down their scale of charges, or by both of these alleviations together.

One great office has, in recent years, taken an important step in the right direction. Formerly the most gross abuses were connected with the collection of premiums and the granting of policies. The ignorant poor were victimised with perfect unscrupulousness and in the most wholesale fashion by collectors, sometimes apparently with the sanction of their employers. Their usual method was to entice people to take out burial money policies, and then, after a few months or a year or two, to allow them to drop out. The collector ceased to call upon them, either because they had changed their place of abode, or simply because he thought he had got all the profit out of the victims he cared for. The "policy" forthwith "lapsed," and the victims had no redress. This system of swindling was prompted by the rule under which collectors received a larger percentage on the earlier than on the later premiums. Sometimes, I believe, the amount granted upon new business, as it was called, was as high as 80 per cent of the first six months' or first year's premiums collected. Naturally, under such a method, dishonest collectors abounded, creatures who devoted the greater part of their energies to new business, to the finding of fresh victims. Such business paid, while the humdrum gathering of pence upon which perhaps 10 or 15 per cent. commission was paid did not yield anything like so comfortable a return, and the office got its share for nothing when the policy was cancelled.

This form of abuse still exists, but is not nearly so rampant as it formerly was, partly because the commissions have been rearranged, partly because the management of the best of these offices has become more honest, careful, and scrupulous ; also, I believe, more solicitous to deal fairly with those who become its clients. Policies do not now " lapse " as they used to do. In the case of the large office alluded to, a system has been adopted of granting fully paid-up policies to people who have paid a certain number of premiums, in the event of their wishing to discontinue their weekly payments or of their inability to keep them up. That meets a sore grievance, formerly universal, viz. the cancelment of policies, no matter how old they were, directly payments were interrupted, or within a few weeks of their interruption. This has now, at least so far as the office I allude to is concerned, become a thing of the past ; but there are other reforms that might very well be attempted, and one of these is the granting of a share in the profits of the business to policy-holders of long standing. At regular periods in the course of the existence of a policy, additions ought to be made to the sums insured representing some fair proportion of the gains that have accrued on it to the insuring company. Several of the offices included in this line of business are wealthy enough to bestow this additional benefit upon their humble clients, and I think they would be well advised to take it into consideration, lest one day something like a revolt against their growing wealth should occur, leading to a demand that they should give an account of their stewardship, or make concessions really perilous to their future solvency.

In other directions modern legislation in the interests, or supposed interests, of the working classes, and new developments arising out of the increasing complexities of modern civilised life, have produced fresh forms of insurance more or less remotely connected with human life. One company, for example, has for many years flourished comfortably upon the insurance of railway passengers during a journey. You buy an in-

D

surance ticket along with your railway ticket, which guarantees the payment of a certain sum down should you unfortunately happen to be killed, or other sums per week for a fixed period in the event of injury. Employers' liability is another description of insurance which has come into existence since the passing of the Employers' Liability Act. It is still, in a manner, in its infancy, gathering its experiences and paying for them. General accident policies can also be obtained from many offices on more or less favourable terms, these terms being to some extent a matter of guess so far as the risks run are concerned, although gradually becoming systematised. Policies are now also granted by many offices to insure the prompt payment of the death duties upon estates. You expect to leave so much money that will call for such and such an amount to satisfy the Inland Revenue authorities, and for a certain premium per annum the insurance office will guarantee an immediate payment of this sum.

Some life offices will, to a certain extent, imitate Lloyd's in enabling any man to take out a policy on another man's life, or will bet at the instance of a speculative individual to pay down so much should some individual named, the king or the queen or any prominent person, die within a fixed time. It would, however, carry me quite beyond the scope of this little treatise to enter into a lengthy description of these purely speculative forms of insurance. All that need be said is that they have their value as, in the language of the market, "hedgings" against risks in other directions. A man may have undertaken some work involving contingent liabilities which he cannot measure and possibility of loss. To partly save himself from this chance of loss he takes out a speculative policy, pays £50 or £100 to the underwriters to secure £1,000 or £5,000, or whatever it may be, in the event of some named individual dying within a given period. It is a favourite method amongst Stock Exchange speculators of trying to protect themselves against the risks of their fascinating but dangerous pursuit.

CHAPTER III

ORDINARY LIFE INSURANCE

SMALL PAID-UP POLICIES

I HAVE often thought, and sometimes said, that our ordinary life companies might solve the difficulty of many people in determining when to take out a life policy, and do an excellent stroke of business for themselves, if they would come down from their lofty perches and condescend to do business for the common people. In 1881 I wrote some articles in the old *Pall Mall Gazette*, discussing the position of life insurance business, and making some animadversions upon the sluggishness and lack of enterprise displayed by most of our English offices. Some of their abuses were also attacked, and I am glad to see that in looking back to those articles no small progress has since been made in various directions. No English company of any standing now cheats clients who may become unable to continue their payments through misfortune by refusing to pay to them any surrender value. Delays no longer form the rule in paying policies when they become claims, and in other directions reforms have taken place. But British offices, English and Scotch, are still much too plutocratic in their modes of doing business, and look with scorn upon the humble individual who might only be able to invest £1 or £5 in a policy.

Because of this aloofness from the common people, we find no British life office doing what is called an "ordinary" life business granting policies below £100. That is the limit of minuteness, and in consequence of this rule, as also of the general refusal to grant single-premium policies except for large amounts, we see the industrial form of business flourish and expand in a manner that ought long ago to have taught the other companies a lesson. Why cannot they take a share in this small business, and open the advantages they undoubtedly can offer to the humble individual earning a modest weekly wage, just as freely as to the struggling clerk who, on a salary of perhaps £2 10s. to £3 a week, tries to save enough to take out a policy of "£100 with profits" payable at death? There seems to me no reason why a splendid business, beneficial to all parties, might not be done by our ordinary life companies in selling single-premium policies for the smallest payments down. A young man might often be able to spare £5 or £10 before the obligations, cares, and expenses of a family come upon his hands, and were it opportunely put before them, thousands of such would, I feel sure, be delighted to hand over their savings to the amount of £5 or £10 or £20 to a reputable and carefully managed life office in exchange for a fully paid "with profits" life policy, becoming due either at death or at a predetermined future date. In this way some provision against the accidents of life might be made at once, without laying upon the policy-holder the burden of perhaps a life-long payment of annual premiums, or a heavier ratio of premium payments for twenty or twenty-five years.

One of our old life offices has recently put forth a scheme, under which it accepts money on deposit at a fixed rate of interest, and treats the capital thus assigned either as a paid-up policy from the first for a like sum repayable practically at any time, or as a basis for an annuity which does not exhaust the capital. That, carefully handled, seems to me a step in the right direction ; but why cannot all our good offices go very much further and sell small policies, as it were, retail without the forms of medical examination or anything else? They could conduct this business at very little expense, and not only make profit for themselves, but for their clients.   Such paid-up policies should be subject in all respects to the rules governing the ordinary level-premium life or endowment policies ; that is to say, policies whose premiums are payable either during the whole period of the insurant's existence, or during ten, fifteen, or twenty years, as may be determined.   The buyer of the policy would understand that he could not claim his money, or any portion of it, back on any consideration before, let us say, three years had elapsed ; but that if he did after a certain number of years require some temporary financial assistance, he could get an advance upon it at a moderate rate of interest, just as upon a policy the weight of whose annual premium might form a burden upon his income all the years of his life.   Or the money paid might be refundable in full on three months' notice, although in that case there would be no question of surrender value in the ordinary sense upon such policies ; but the offices would have to protect themselves against loss of working expenses, by stipulating that if the money were returned within, say, three years, no interest or accumulated "profits" would be allowed. After that date the proportion of the accumulation at compound interest assigned to the policy might be held back were the principal required to be refunded, and given the form of a fixed policy payable at death. In essence, a life policy of this kind simply represents a deposit at compound interest, out of which the office granting it would make a small profit to cover current expenses and the original commission, which should be small, paid upon the business. But the mode might be varied so as to prevent the policy-holder from having free scope for the display of his selfishness in moments of pressure. The money might be held for five, ten, or twenty years, or for life, just as if the policies were of the ordinary sort.

Were this system of single-payment policies for small sums adopted, there would be no question with any man as to when he should take out a policy other than whether he had any money to do it with or not. At any period of life a man possessed of £5 to spare might lock it up in this fashion with great advantage, always assuming that the office he goes to is an honest one, conducted with vigilance and business acumen. When one considers the enormous difficulties thrown in the way of small thrift in this country, the surprise grows all the more that some such method of business has not been adopted by our life offices long ago. They could have cut out Post Office insurance, and to a large extent industrial assurance, by systematically devoting themselves to the cultivation of the small saver, or the classes who know nothing about stocks and shares, or who frequently lose their money by indiscreet or heedless excursions into the region of the Stock Exchange.

There is but one danger of a formidable, not to say insurmountable, nature that presents itself on turning over in one's mind a plan of this kind, and it is that the offices doing the paid-up small policy business might become so rich as to have difficulty in knowing how to invest profitably the funds committed to their care. We may be sure, however, that they would exercise a vigilance in putting away the funds rolling in upon them which ninety-nine out of every hundred private investors are incapable of doing for themselves, because of their ignorance and unacquaintance with the share

market, and sometimes because of their uninstructed cupidity. Had our life offices stepped
in between the company promoter and the small
investor in this manner years ago, I cannot but
think that great numbers of people would now
have something laid aside against evil days to
come who, as they stand, are stripped bare. To
be sure, the scope for investment is not endless.
The world cannot go on for ever creating new
securities, piling up debts upon the backs of the
workers, mortgaging the wealth of the many to
the few, multiplying obligations of every description for which the toilers are alone ultimately
responsible, or joint-stocking every form of investment that the ingenuity of man can invent. True
as that is, the scope is practically infinite still, and
for generations to come must continually widen,
widen quite sufficiently to prevent a business of
this description, however large, from coming to a
natural end for want of any security to yield interest. In our own country, were the landlords to
become men of wisdom and open up the soil to the
small owner-cultivator on equitable terms, to sell
their property to such in handy lots, scope for
mortgage business within the United Kingdom
alone would be sufficient to absorb the savings of

several generations of the thrifty. And the wealth need not roll up with any alarming rapidity, because there would always be claims coming forward. Money would be dispersed as well as accumulated, so that although the growth of assets would certainly be rapid beyond anything known to the jog-along, eminently respectable life office familiar to us, it would not grow faster with any of them than the rate of accumulations shown by some of our industrial offices. I commend this idea to the enterprising men amongst life insurance managers. They might not only widen their business enormously by stepping out, but cut the ground from under the feet of many of the specious alien offices, full of flaming advertisement of their wonderful juggleries in finance, and gradually succeed in keeping at home, for the fertilisation of domestic industries, most of the savings now flowing out of the country, too often through channels that drain it to waste.

CHAPTER IV

HOW AND WHEN TO INSURE

I. HOW

SUPPOSING you have decided to take out a life policy of the orthodox stamp, the questions of greatest importance to be determined are, how the form of the policy shall be settled, and where it will be wisest to go to purchase it. A good deal has been said already on the former of these subjects, but there is plenty of scope for further observations. Whether is it wiser, for instance, to take an "endowment" policy or a "whole life" policy? The former involves, as already explained, the payment of a heavier premium, but only for a term of years, the latter means payment as long as one lives. Circumstances must determine the choice, but my prepossession is in favour of a policy whose premium payments shall end within a fixed term of years. Various reasons and some personal experience incline me to give this

44

preference.   Not only is it well to avoid liabilities in old age, but it is better to have a term fixed on the arrival of which the policy-holder can make up his mind what is to be done with the accumulated money.   I think that a man should always have this power in his lifetime.   If policies payable only after death are taken out in youth, it is impossible to foresee the circumstances which may exist twenty or thirty years later.   A man who insured under the age of thirty, with a view to provide for his family, may in old age have no family to provide for.   His circumstances may be such that it would be better for him to invest his available capital in an annuity for the remainder of his life, or for the joint lives of himself and his wife, than to go on bearing the burden of a life-policy premium with a view to make provision for some people—he may not quite know whom—coming forward as claimants after his death.

No doubt these policies whose premiums run for a term of years can be turned to selfish uses. A man with a family may be tempted to neglect the interests of that family and apply the capital accrued under the policy wholly or partly to his own uses ; but, after all, that is a matter which must be determined by individual tastes and idiosyncrasies. Moreover, it is always possible, if a policy has been of any important size, to adjust interests so that the coming generation's wants may be to some extent satisfied as well as those of the policy-holder in his old age. Most life offices of repute will be quite willing to set aside either the capital sum originally insured or some portion thereof to be paid at the insurant's death to his heirs, and devote the balance to founding an annuity for the said insurant during his life. They may not do this in a generous spirit some of them, but in a spirit of short-sighted niggardliness ; still they will all, to some extent, modify the contract. Any way, I have long thought the level-premium payment during a whole life a mistake. It is still the most popular form of life policy, judging by the returns of the various life offices, but that is probably because these offices continue to cultivate this form of policy with the greatest assiduity. They put it first before those they are seeking to persuade to insure their lives. It looks so much cheaper, too, the premium rates being lower, and also I think it is certainly more profitable to the offices issuing it. But that is no reason why intelligent people should simply do as they are told in this matter. A life policy should never be taken out rashly, least of all a policy involving a liability for every year that a man lives. Failing the paid-up policy bought with a single premium, I think the shorter the period a man burdens himself with payments of this kind the better, provided he be a careful and prudent person, as I assume all my readers are, or wish to become.

Another question to be settled beforehand is whether the policy should be with profits or without. It is really a matter of indifference to most people, or a matter of payment and convenience. Strictly speaking, under the scientific method of conducting life insurance business so thoroughly well established, no such thing as " profit," in the usual sense of the word, comes into the case. All that the insurant who buys a " with profit " policy gets is a prearranged share in the compound interest accumulated on the invested moneys, which share he pays for. Actuaries are able to tell to a penny how much they can give in exchange for so much premium by way of bonus upon a fixed sum insured. You take out a policy for £1,000 without profits, and the premium is so much smaller than that payable upon a similar policy taken out with profits. There is the whole secret. The extra money paid in by you accumulated at compound interest, less "loading," a term I shall presently explain, is your "profit."

Being thus a matter of payment, it really becomes for each individual who means to take out a life policy a question of what he can afford. At any rate it should be so, but there are some offices that throw tempting baits before people they wish to ensnare, such baits representing in many cases mere estimates of imaginary profits which are never, or rarely ever, fulfilled, and in others an assumption of a higher rate of interest than reasonable probabilities warrant over a term of years. Suppose, for example, a life office has been in the habit of looking to accumulate its money at $4\frac{1}{2}$ per cent. compound interest, and that hitherto that expectation has been justified and more, it may be able for a time to promise and to pay a higher scale of profits on with profit policies than its neighbour whose management reckons on accumulating its funds at only 3 per cent. compound interest. The premium of the $4\frac{1}{2}$ per cent. office may be as low as, or even lower than, that of the office working upon what is called a 3 per cent. basis of accumulation, and yet the promise of gains may be higher. It does not follow, however,

that the office promising the most is in the long
run the safest.   The time may come, generally
does, when it is no longer able to obtain an
average of $4\frac{1}{2}$ per cent. net upon its invested funds,
and when that day does arrive it may bring
trouble, because the office is only too likely to
strain to keep up appearances.

Those whose policies have become claims in the
meantime will have gained, but the new insurants
who have come forward and taken their places
may have to bear the losses.   The funds, that is to
say, will have been depleted by the earlier distri-
butions upon policies becoming claims, so that, in
order to recover lost ground, the holders of newer
policies will have to be content with smaller
" profits."   Much play, however, may be made by
help of what may be called surprise profits.   An
office bases its estimates on a 3 per cent. rate of
accumulation and actually makes $4\frac{1}{4}$ per cent.
The difference becomes excess profit, and enables
bonuses above forecasts to be declared.   An element of what looks like speculation can thus be
made to enter into the business, and must not be
lost sight of.   Partly for that reason I am disposed
to think that the with profits form of policy should
not be so generally run after as it is.   It seems to

E

me better that a man should insure a net sum and be done with it. At the same time there is always the attraction to ordinary human nature of a little unforeseen gain, a something received beyond what was stipulated for or promised ; and there may be no harm in gratifying this instinct, I may call it, provided a first-class office is selected. With endowment policies, indeed, the profit-sharing system is perhaps for most people the best, because it forces them to put aside a little more money than they otherwise might do, but in the case of life-long premium payments it is not infrequently otherwise. These often become irksome as time goes on, and the compensating advantage of profit to one's heirs is not always visible. The worst of it is that the profits seem as much locked up as the amount of the policy ; but I shall return to that when we come to deal with surrender values.

2. WHEN

The younger the better, one might answer offhand, and pass on to another subject, but that would be too summary a treatment of a really important matter. It is quite true that the young should make a certain provision against the chances of life at as early an age as they can, because the premiums to be paid are smaller when one is young than when up in years. A young man of twenty-one can, in most offices, get a life policy of £100 with profits, payable at death, for a payment of about £2 per annum—in some cases it is a little less, in others a little more—whereas at thirty he will have to pay from £2 5s. to £2 10s., and at forty the premium will run from £2 15s. to upwards of £3 10s. per annum. Multiply this by fives or tens to get at the premiums on heavier insurances, and it will be obvious what the advantages of early insurance are.

But should all young men, and in these days young women also, effect insurance on their lives? I cannot positively answer "yes," but am quite sure that no obvious reason exists why they should not, provided they have the means. The only point to be looked to, let me again insist, is not to over-insure. It is an easy matter to take out a fresh policy later on, as and if means improve, but it is never wise for the young to hamper themselves with excessive payments when their spare means may be better employed in other directions. After all, life insurance in any form should be looked upon merely as a provision for the unexpected and unforeseen. It is a mistake, and sometimes little short of a crime against one's family, to treat it as a substitute for every other form of thrift, as too many do, with the result that they cultivate self-indulgence in all other directions instead of economy. Most people will know examples illustrative of this habit, know men who, because they have taken out policies likely to bring £1,000, or a few thousands, to their family at death, spend every other penny they earn, and make no attempt at economy in any direction. That is not the way to treat life insurance. It is fair neither to oneself nor to one's dependants. The object aimed at should be a moderate provision against the unforeseen and unforeseeable. That provision made, there is no occasion to go further, and the limit should never be so high as first to hamper, and then to lead to the disregard of, other forms of thrift.

I have been speaking thus far of whole life policies. The case is somewhat altered when we turn to the fashionable endowment system, where a man contracts to pay an enhanced premium for say fifteen or twenty years and then to be done with it. When this form of assurance is adopted, then the middle period of life seems to be the best time to insure. That is to say, a man aged between thirty and fifty, presumably at his best as

a worker, should be in the most favoured position
for sparing a considerable sum out of his income
in order to effect a substantial insurance as provision for old age, or for those who come after
him, or for both. Life offices, however, generally
arrange their scales of premiums so that younger
clients can spread their payments over a longer
term of years than those who are older. For
example, a man at the age of twenty-five can
arrange to spread his endowment policy payments
over thirty, thirty-five, or forty years if he pleases,
so that his premiums will cease when he is fifty-
five, sixty, or sixty-five ; whereas a man at the age
of forty cannot possibly hope, on the average expectation of life, to continue endowment payments
for anything like so long a period as thirty-five,
still less for forty years. His periods should therefore range between fifteen and twenty-five years,
so that he also will cease paying at the utmost
when he is sixty-five. Now a policy of £1,000
taken out by the man at the age of twenty-five,
the premium upon which will cease in thirty years,
will cost between £30 and £40 per annum, according to the office selected, whereas a similar policy
payable in fifteen years taken out by a man aged
forty will cost on an average quite £70 per annum,

and even if payable over a period of twenty-five years, the outlay will represent from £40 to £50 per annum.

Why, it may be asked, should there be such differences between the premiums charged by various offices for an identical article? Some of the best of them, for instance, charge apparently the highest scales of premium. Is there any advantage in paying the high figure rather than the low? or is the office that offers to insure the £1,000 at the lowest scale the best to go to? I shall deal with this matter of cost further on, and in the meantime need only observe that the mere scale of premium taken by itself is not necessarily an indication that the policy on which a higher scale is charged is dearer than one on which the premium is lower, if a share in the profits is included in the policy. Where no profits are granted there ought to be, and is, much less difference between the scales charged by different offices for the same class of policy. Even there, however, differing conditions as to payment, etc., may quite legitimately cause a slight divergence, and the mere fact that one office exacts a somewhat higher scale of premium than another ought not to cause such office to be rejected by intending insurants, unless something else intervenes to bar out the dearer office.

Another matter which should help to determine the insurant as to when he will take up a life policy is the purpose he has in view.   If he aims at providing a sum at his death for those dependent upon him he should certainly begin modestly, let me again insist, if young, and rather multiply his policies as he gets older and wealthier, always within moderate limits, than load himself up at the start with a heavy annual liability.   As men grow older the law of wisdom changes.   In middle age it is probably best to invest in as heavy a life policy as one can carry, and as a rule it should be an endowment policy.   Much will depend upon circumstances always.   Where a man's position is secure—say, a good income with a retiring allowance at the end of the day's work—there may often be little call for a life policy of any size or character ; but where a man has to look forward to reduced working powers and diminished income, let him load up when in his strength to the full extent of his ability.   It is always, in my opinion, wisest to invest in an endowment policy in such circumstances, a policy so framed that payments thereon will cease before old age begins to tell on the working powers. It should further be a policy so framed that its fruits can be utilised as circumstances demand, either to provide the owner with an annuity from a fixed future date, or with a lump sum down if he so pleases, or, as yet another alternative, to give his heirs at death a stipulated amount with bonuses. An elderly man, in short, should so arrange his life assurance as to be able to deal with the proceeds of his policy or policies at maturity according to his own necessities or those of persons dependent upon him. Should an insurant have no one to bestow the capital upon by will, then the money can probably be always best employed in creating an annuity for one or more lives—for the holder and his wife. On grounds like these, I think that a man who waits until of a comparatively mature age should take up as heavy a policy or group of endowment policies as can be afforded. But one should never wait till old age dries up energies and perhaps the sources of income before seeking to insure. The provision of money either for old age or against premature death is a duty for the young or comparatively young. When old it is too late except in one form, a form becoming dearer with every month that passes. A man up in years may buy, at a price which looks cheap, a policy guaranteeing a certain sum to his heirs, provided he dies within twelve months, or two years, or three, but that is an expensive form of betting satisfactory to nobody. Hence it is best always to begin early with life insurance.

CHAPTER V

WHERE TO INSURE

I. THE NEED FOR CAUTION

OF all questions that must be determined, where to insure is the most vital. Nothing is more calamitous than a false step in this business, and unfortunately false steps are the easiest possible to take—much more easy, I am sorry to say, in our days than they formerly were. No doubt we have had bad insurance companies in the past, and some very lamentable failures; but considering the number of people engaged in the business, the immunity from outside criticism or efficient inspection and the slow growth of facts scientifically collated, of accumulated actuarial experience, and the temptation of delusive investments, it is wonderful how little suffering has been inflicted upon the people of this country by life companies of good repute. In the present day, however, dangers of many new kinds beset the path of the man who is desirous of making some reliable provision for the future, either for his own old age or for those who come after him, by this method of investment. Not only have great plausibilities in new forms of temptation been invented or faked up, but offices of very doubtful quality have pushed themselves forward, and in some cases have succeeded in obtaining a large share of the life business done year after year in the United Kingdom. The pitfalls which beset people when they come to insure their lives are therefore numerous and often well concealed. Hence I shall have a good deal to say upon this subject, because it is the most important and vital of all. Not only is it a vexatious thing and a cruel misfortune that the, often painfully set aside, life premiums, by the investment of which a man hoped to shield those dependent upon him from sudden misfortune, should be dissipated and utilised simply for the profit and glorification of designing adventurers, but it is portentous of disaster to the public. Therefore I propose to lay down a series of rules which every individual who seeks to insure his life ought to follow, not merely if he wishes to make a profitable investment, but if he desires to escape vexation and possible loss.

2. INSURE AT HOME

The first of these rules is to this effect—NEVER INSURE IN ANY LIFE OFFICE WHOSE HEAD-QUARTERS ARE NOT IN THE UNITED KINGDOM. That I regard as an essential preliminary. At the present time there are United States offices and several colonial of many qualities—some of them perhaps good enough, one or two excellent, others the reverse of good—striving to do business in this country, and with no small success. My advice is—disregard them all, and look to home offices alone. Quite a number of reasons may be given in support of this counsel, but at present I will mention only one or two that can be understood by everybody, and the most prominent of these is that all foreign offices are totally outside the control of policy-holders here. In the event of anything going wrong, such policy-holders have neither adequate legal remedy nor tangible hold over such assets as there may be. They cannot effectively move the English courts of justice, put in receivers to nurse or preserve the assets; they cannot intervene to check abuses, nor have they any voice whatever in determining the channels into which the money they contribute shall flow.

Surely these alone are reasons sufficient to prevent people of sense from committing their savings
in the quarters indicated. It is quite true that
these offices become subject to our Board of Trade
rules when they do business in this country, but
it is the misfortune of Englishmen to get no
efficient protection from their administrative departments in matters of business, and such protection as offers covers only business done here or
assets within the kingdom.

After the failure of the Albert and European
Life Offices in 1869, about which I had something
to say at the start, there was a great disturb-
ance and upset of the public mind which could
only be satisfied by legislation. Our law-makers
duly set to work to frame regulations that would
in their opinion prevent anything like imposture
or misappropriation of funds, and guard the insured against directorial stupidity in the years to
come. An Act was duly passed in 1871, under
which all life offices doing business in this country
were compelled to render their accounts in one
particular form and to report every year in this
form to the Board of Trade. Good was done,
doubtless, by this proviso, as also by the stipula-
tion that no insurance company or association

whatever issuing life policies should be allowed to begin business here until it had deposited £20,000 with the Board of Trade as a sort of guarantee of good faith. But the Act omitted altogether to give the Board of Trade any administrative control over the conduct of a business once started. If any curious person takes the trouble to turn up in a public library or elsewhere the annual reports of the life companies, issued by the Board of Trade as a blue-book, almost the first thing that will strike even a cursory reader is the absolute helplessness of this department to check abuses. It can write letters and demonstrate that wrong is being done and criticise, but there its power ends. All that a mere group of swindlers have to do, therefore, is to beg, borrow, or steal £20,000, deposit that money with the Board of Trade, and then start upon their depredations without let or hindrance.

A life office may be insolvent, it may practise the most disgraceful tricks in order to cheat the innocent and ignorant multitude, and the law can do nothing, or at least those who ought to be the administrators of the law stand helpless. You as an individual, or a dozen individuals together, may club money and prosecute, but officialism does nothing, having no real power to do anything.

3. PROPRIETARY AND MUTUAL OFFICES

Having ruled out alien offices of all descriptions, the next thing an intelligent citizen should do is to enter upon an examination of the position of home offices. It does not require any elaborate preparation in order to do this to an extent sufficient for the object in view, so that there is no call to jib about this advice and be afraid of it. *Never trust to the statements of eager canvassers, but look into things for yourself.* Every year accounts are issued in a stated form which will enable anyone who desires to take out a life policy of any description to ascertain in a fairly satisfactory manner the kind of business done, the quality of the investments held by the office or company, the ratio of expenses to the premium income, and other vital matters of that description.

At the outset it will be found that two classes of offices, both good, compete for the favour of the public. The one class is " proprietary," a company with shareholders, that is, whose capital requires a dividend ; and the other is called " mutual," where there is no share capital, and the only stored resources consist of the moneys accumulated from policy-holders and invested during the years of the office's existence. At first sight it might seem that the most economical course to follow would be to contract for a policy from a mutual office, but there is really very little, if any, difference between the two classes of offices, if the good ones alone are looked to.

Formerly there was a good deal of difference, and the public owes it to the mutual offices that many abuses, prevalent in the old days with the joint-stock company insurance offices, have been remedied. The most flagrant of these abuses, so far as the public was concerned, lay in the freedom enjoyed by shareholders to appropriate whatever slices of the profits seemed to them good. If a company had a fat year or group of fat years, whether through successful traffic in investments, or through the smallness of the death rate, or from any cause, it was open to the directors to appropriate the bulk of this extra profit to their shareholders and to leave the so-called profit-sharing policy-holders with no more than the usual pittance, with little or no share of the extra gain. Without elaborating this part of a now almost forgotten past history, it may at once be stated that joint-stock insurance offices of repute now generally limit the share assigned to proprietors to, at the most, 10 per cent.

of the profits from all sources. Sometimes this
may look a large sum, but, generally speaking, it
amounts to a very small tax upon the revenue
coming from life business, and sometimes to almost
no tax at all. This is especially the case where
funds have been accumulated out of past heavy
profits and laid by in the interest of the proprietors
alone. It happens occasionally in these cases that
the interest upon proprietors' funds, so called,
is more than sufficient to yield an ample dividend upon the paid-up share capital, for, generally speaking, such share capital is quite small. A
life company, once well started, requires very little
money beyond the statutory deposit of £20,000,
and one, at least, of the big offices has built up its
now magnificent capital totally out of the past
profits, money furnished by insurants. One other
old and excellent office possesses a share capital
of only £5,000, it having begun business long
before the Act of 1871.

4. THE TEST OF ECONOMY

Such being the position, it is unnecessary to
devote much attention to the status of an office,
to ask whether it be joint-stock or mutual. *The
one thing to settle first of all is whether the*
F

business is economically conducted or not. But how can an outsider know this? In a rough and ready but, practically, quite efficient way, with no difficulty whatever, merely by doing one of the simplest sums in division a School Board teacher would set to a child in the third or fourth standard. Take on the one hand the premium income as set forth in the revenue and expenditure account of the latest year available, and on the other the cost of management and commissions. In arriving at the expenditure, include everything paid out for running the business except, perhaps, the income tax, which is not an expenditure within the control of the office and should be left out. Where exceptional bad debts or losses are shown, such items may also be omitted, but sums written off furniture etc., should be included. Add all such items of expenditure together and then divide the total by the amount of the net premium income, adding two noughts to the total of the expenses, and the quotient will be the ratio per cent. of the premium income absorbed in current outgoings, otherwise the actual amount of the "loading" for expenses.

Assume, by way of example, the net premium income—the income after deducting reassurance —to be £369,432, as set forth in the accounts, and the expenses under all heads to total £41,865, the sum to be done is the following :—

$$369432\overline{)4186500}(11\cdot33$$
$$369432$$
$$\overline{492180}$$
$$369432$$
$$\overline{1227480}$$
$$1108296$$
$$\overline{1191840}$$
$$1108296$$
$$\overline{83544}$$

That is to say, the cost of working the business comes out at 11·33 per cent., which may be deemed a fair average rate. It is unnecessary to carry the calculation beyond the second decimal.

If the ratio should be high, leave the office whose extravagance is in this way proved severely alone. Some of our older offices pay no commission whatever to agents for bringing them new clients, and are able consequently to work their business at a very small proportion of the income from premiums, 7 to 8 per cent. as a rule. The bulk, however, of what may be called progressive offices all pay commissions to those who canvass the public for them, and they are compelled to do so if their business is to show steady expansion. It may be taken as an invariable rule that an office which does not pay those who bring business to it for their trouble is a stagnant office. It may be extremely rich, generally is, an office thoroughly well worth taking out a policy in, but, thanks to the apathy of the public, it is passed by for offices whose canvassers go into the highways and by-ways and lug candidates for life policies in, as it were, by the scruff of the neck.

As the habit is to pay a heavier percentage of commission on the first premium, or few premiums, received as product of a canvasser's success in capturing clients, it follows that an office whose business reveals large expansion every year will show at the same time a higher ratio of expenses to the total premium income than one whose business is non-progressive. To be strictly just, therefore, the cost of the new business ought to be ascertained separately from that of the old, but often this cannot be done because of the insufficiency of the figures supplied. They are not always split up in a manner that enables a mere outsider to get at the facts. It is enough, however, for all practical purposes to get the general ratio of expenditure to the entire premium income, that is to say, the premium income remaining with the office after it has paid for reassuring parts of its risks, the "net" premium income. Proceeding in this way, it will be found that the working outlay of really good offices ranges between 10 and 15 or at the utmost 16 per cent. of the premium income, and I have always advised that policies should not be taken out with any office whose expenses, year in and out, run beyond 16 per cent. of the premium income. Many people have alleged that this is too hard and fast a rule, and that young offices struggling to be great, compelled to be in the fashion and to gratify the passion of the multitude for bigness, must frequently expend more than 17 per cent. of their premium income in order to forge ahead. It may be so ; I do not wish to act the part of a censor. All I contend for is that the prudent man who desires to have a good sheet-anchor in the shape of a substantial life policy or endowment policy, put forth against unpleasant and unforeseen adversities, should look to the first-class offices alone to give him what he requires. And an office which spends on the average of years much more than £15 out of every £100 received as premiums on policies in current outgoings is not an economical office, no matter how strong it may be in a financial sense for the time being.

Many of the offices that do fire and other classes of business as well as life insurance limit the amount they expend on the life department to 10 per cent. of the premium income. Other purely life offices bring their figures very nearly down to that percentage; but it is hardly possible for even the best of commission-giving offices to reduce their expenses much below 12 per cent. of the premium income, if they are to hold their own and obtain the requisite share of the new business, and those who intend to insure must make up their minds to pay a fair price for the contract they enter into. It is the public's own fault that the business is so costly. Could a man be certain of living the full term of his life, there would be no necessity for him to insure, that is to say, presuming him to be a prudent man, and men too often treat the subject as if long life were a certainty for them. They must pay for their indifference. By putting aside every year so much of his income, and allowing it to accumulate at compound interest, a man sure of living long would doubtless be better off at the end of twenty or thirty years than any insurance office could make him. Recognising, however, the uncertainty of life, and also bearing in mind that the intricate and responsible business of collecting premiums and investing funds, watching over markets, and protecting interests of great complexity and magnitude is a business that cannot be conducted for nothing, no reasonable man will refuse to pay fairly for the services rendered.

5. THE NATURE OF THE INVESTMENTS HELD

Having found an office whose rate of expenditure is not excessive, the next thing to look at is the character of its investments. Much depends upon that whether the contract will be in the end fulfilled or not. The stand-by of all British offices is mortgages upon real estate, and some of them confine their loans on this class of security to property within the United Kingdom. Others do a large mortgage business in the colonies, and some combine with that alien business the deposit of money in colonial banks, although this last is not a practice anything like so common now as it was before the collapse of Australian banks in 1893.

Is this mortgage class of security safe? As a rule, yes, although, like everything else, if it is too exclusively leaned upon it is apt to fail and to involve those who have lent the money in loss. British offices, for instance, that have lent large amounts of money on Irish land, have for many years been obliged to contemplate the possibility of having to write off considerable sums as irrecoverable. Some of them probably have already done this on the quiet, saying nothing about it. Great, therefore, is the relief afforded to them by the latest Irish Land Act.

As years have gone on, however, the variety of securities offering for money collected by life offices has enormously expanded, and nowadays it is common enough to see life offices putting their gatherings into all manner of what are called "marketable securities" which in former days would have been given the go-by. There is, for example, the immense class of bonds and other securities issued by the United States Railroads. Also there are hundreds of millions of stocks issued by the Railways of India, as well as by the Government of India and by Colonial State Governments. Our own municipalities, likewise, have fallen into the debt-piling fashion, and during little more than a generation have created obligations to the amount of something like £300,000,000, and the

total is always being added to. We have furthermore our Home Railways with their debenture
and preference guaranteed stocks, to the tune
of nearly £700,000,000 ; and there are immense
numbers of industrial or manufacturing joint-stock
companies that have important debenture or preference share issues, some of which have proved
tempting to insurance offices. Take a glance
through life offices' lists of investments, then, and
note whether any office has an apparently excessive amount in any one class of security. All
have their risks, and the only way to avoid danger
of heavy loss in any one direction is to so distribute
the investments that the risk in a particular class of
security will not be excessive in proportion to the
rest.

Picking up, almost at random, the balance sheet
of a life office whose total assets exceed £4,000,000,
I find, for example, that out of this imposing sum
nearly £900,000 is invested in Home Railway debentures and other stocks, over £750,000 in Indian
and Colonial State Government and Colonial Provincial securities, and upwards of £500,000 in
mortgages on property within the United Kingdom, the balance being distributed over a variety
of classes of securities, such as mortgages on life

interests or on reversions, mortgages on county and corporation rates, loans on the office's own policies within their surrender value, freehold property, British Government securities, and so on. Is this list a fairly safe one? I think it is. There may be a little too much money in domestic railway securities, especially if a large amount of it is in the ordinary or unprotected stocks, but on the whole the list, as far as its mere summary of investments goes, seems to be a thoroughly good one.

Take another example, however, from an office whose total assets exceed £12,500,000, and here we find nearly £5,500,000 of the total sunk in mortgages, some £3,000,000 of it on property within the United Kingdom, and nearly £2,250,000 on property outside the kingdom. Here we should say the proportion of the money invested in one particular class of security is excessive, especially that sunk in mortgages outside the United Kingdom. Is this company, then, in a weak position? By no means, but its position is such that its controllers ought to devote a considerable sum every year in order to provide against the possibility of losses upon a class of investments difficult to control, and wholly unrealisable in mass at all times. It should have a reserve, not merely hidden,

but openly displayed, so as to add to the confidence of its clients. In other respects its figures
are quite satisfactory. I do not even object to
find nearly £2,000,000 of the money sunk in
United States sterling and gold bonds, for the
higher classes of these bonds seem to be amongst
the best securities in the world.

Yet another large office whose assets exceed
£5,000,000 has upwards of £1,000,000 in mortgages on property within the United Kingdom,
and nearly £2,750,000 in railway stocks of various
descriptions, including preference and ordinary.
Here again I should say that the amount sunk in
railway securities is disproportionate, and that it
would be more satisfactory to policy-holders to
see the money scattered over a greater variety
of classes of stocks. It must, however, be can-
didly admitted that the law as it stands does not
compel life offices to give a sufficiently full list of
their investments to enable definite opinions to be
expressed. All one can say is that the purchases
or placements seem to have run too much in one
direction, but it does not follow that the investments of that particular group are not in themselves good or of the best. I should like to see
all life office investments set forth in detail, some-

what after the fashion ordered by the legislature of the State of New York and of other States in the North American Union. There each security is named and the amount of the investment therein set forth in full, so that it is possible for those who wish to insure to find out without much trouble whether the money appears to be properly put aside or not. Even the American system, however, as thus illustrated is not perfect, and I think a valuable reform at home would be one which obliged the life offices to set forth in detail every security possessed by them, together with the cost price and the actual market value at the date of the balance sheet.

Passing this point by as a matter to some extent open to controversy, the broad rule to be observed by those in quest of an office with which to effect a life or endowment policy is that any British office which has the bulk of its securities invested in property or stocks of the United Kingdom is on the whole safer than one that goes far afield. This is especially the case with mortgages upon real estate abroad, the quality of which is apt to fluctuate in a manner surprising to those who have never given the subject any study, and I should give the preference to an office

which has no excessive or disproportionate mass
of its funds in any one class of security, however
good, not even in Home Railway stocks or in
Home mortgages.

6. SURRENDER VALUES

Having ascertained these points, it is then
necessary to go on and find out what the treatment of the insured is by the particular offices.
This does not vary nowadays so much as it once
did. Upwards of twenty years ago now, when I
had occasion to animadvert a good deal upon the
shortcomings of our life offices in regard to their
clients, the abuses were numerous. Many of the
offices were extremely tardy in meeting claims
after they had become due owing to the death of
the policy-holder ; others took an excessive proportion of the profits accruing on with profit
policies ; others charged too high premiums and
gave too little in return ; and above all there was
shameful niggardliness in the matter of surrender
values. Some of these imperfections remain,
notably the difficulty that often arises over the
dates of birth when policies become claims.

What is a surrender value? It is simple
enough. Let us suppose that you have taken out

a life policy for £1,000, and that, after say ten years, circumstances make it impossible for you to continue to pay the premiums on this policy. Assuming the premium to have been £25 per annum, in the course of ten years you will have given the office whose policy you purchased £250, and furthermore will have sacrificed the interest which this money might have been earning if deposited by you as saved. On the other hand, the life office has been enjoying the use of this money all the time and, less the 10 to 15 per cent. of it absorbed in current expenses, will have been accumulating the profit upon the balance invested by it at 4 per cent. or 3 per cent. per annum. The £250 will therefore have become perhaps £320, perhaps more, in the hands of the life office, all deductions, or "loadings," as they are called, for expenses allowed for. When your inability to continue paying the premium compels you to go to the life office in quest of relief, the question to be determined is what proportion of this money the office will hand you back on the cancellation of the contract. In former days some of the offices gave nothing at all, others in a more or less niggardly fashion threw back insignificant, some-times derisory, amounts and sent the unfortunate client away with a grudge against life insurance in all its forms.

There has been a considerable reform in this respect in recent years, but a good deal has to be done still, and I know but few offices which frankly set forth at the time the policy is taken out the surrender value it will carry after each year of life. This could be done by all of them without the slightest difficulty. To avoid doing it is, therefore, to pave the way for deceptions, and it may be, in some cases, to make considerable sums of money at the expense of the policy-holders. These policy-holders naturally do not understand the subject, and through not understanding it many of them probably advance unreasonable demands. They forget two important considerations which the actuary must take into account in determining the proportion of the money paid in that can be handed back without injuring the other policy-holders or loss to the company. The first relates to the cost of working the business. Most offices that give commissions to those who procure business for them pay over as commission a larger percentage of the first premium or first two or three premiums than they do in after years for the mere collection of the stipulated amounts as they fall due. Some extravagant offices hand over as commission 50 per cent., 60 per cent., and even more of the first year's premium to the man through whose agency the policy is effected. Afterwards the commissions may amount to only $2\frac{1}{2}$ per cent., or at most 5 per cent., of the premiums received. In addition there is the regular current expenditure of the office on its establishment—board of directors, upper officials, general staff, office rent, and so forth. This may amount to from 5 to 10 or even 15 per cent., according as the management is lavish or economical; but whatever its amount, this expenditure has to be deducted from the money received as premiums, and the balance alone is left for investment. If the insurant becomes unable within a period of five or six years to continue his payments, it must be obvious that the office whose policy he holds cannot afford to give back so large a proportion of the money received by it as it could do were the policy ten or twenty years old. It has spent a disproportionately large part of the premiums collected in paying first commissions, and the effect of such heavy disbursement is but gradually obliterated by the continuance of payments over a long series of years. The surrender value of a policy must accordingly be small for a young policy compared with the sum disbursed by the policy-holder.

The other point which the policy-holder almost invariably overlooks is his share in the general risk.

It has already been pointed out that the business of life insurance depends upon averages—the average duration of life, the average rate of interest on the money invested, and so on. The life office that issues a policy knows now with mathematical precision what the risk it undertakes amounts to ; that is to say, an approximately certain proportion of its policy-holders will die, or a preascertained minimum number of fixed period policies will become claims within the current twelve months. These various claims fall upon the general funds provided by all the insured, and every new policy-holder in entering into a contract with a life office undertakes his share of this average liability. The office must put aside so much of the money it receives in order to provide for this liability, and as long as the policy endures its holder must bear a well-defined proportion of the expenditure the claims falling in throw upon the office. It follows that a man who is unable to continue his premium

G

payments cannot expect to get back the whole of the balance of his money after working expenses, commissions, and so on have been provided for. Asssume that 10 per cent. of his premiums are on the average required to be set aside to accumulate at compound interest in order to meet the charge continually imposed by the falling due of claims, then that amount must clearly be deducted from the premiums paid in addition to the current expenditure.

Suffer me to illustrate this point somewhat more fully. Let me assume that you have taken out a policy for £1,000 at the age of thirty, and that this policy is one of 2,000 similar contracts entered into by the office. According to the tabulated experiences of life compiled by the Institute of Actuaries, and known as the Hm. (healthy male) and Hf. (healthy female) tables, the deaths to be expected within a year among the 2,000 policy-holders of a like age with yours will number, let us say, thirty-six. The office must therefore lay its account with having to find about £36,000 in the twelve months in order to meet claims on its policies arising through death. The whole of this charge does not fall upon current premiums, because previously received premiums covering policies already in

existence have been invested and are accumulating
at compound interest, but a proportion does, and
the proportion is naturally heavier in the earlier
years of a policy than in the later, when compound
interest tells in accumulating funds over and above
the product of hoarded net premiums against the
liability on the policy. Whatever the risks may be,
as determined by the experience of the office, the
range of its business, the average age of its policies,
etc., a percentage of the accretions of premiums and
compound interest has to be reserved against them,
but in time the accumulations should more than
cover all risks and leave the office with a profit.

It follows that the net amount coming back to
the policy-holder out of the premiums paid must
be small in proportion to the youth of the policy.
Therefore in the early years of its existence the
policy cannot have a large surrender value even in
the best and most carefully conducted life office.
On the other hand, as the years pass the net
amount available for the policy ought to increase,
not merely through the continued payments of
premiums, but by the accumulation at compound
interest, and there can be no difficulty whatever in
determining to a shilling what this amount is after
all risks have been calculated and allowed for. It

follows that every life office which conducts its business on honourable lines is at any moment in a position to say what the real surrender value of a policy amounts to, and there is no reason whatever why tables of surrender values should not be as common in life insurance offices' prospectuses as tables of premiums.

Some of the most enlightened and progressive offices do supply such tables and find the custom to their advantage, but the great bulk of them still hesitate to take this step and leave their clients in the dark. This ought not to be the case. From one point of view, life insurance is simply a method of laying up savings, and it ought not to be so costly a method as it too often proves to be, to those who become unable to continue premium payments, if the business is properly conducted, and as the actual surrender value grudgingly doled out by many important offices on old standing policies would lead one to infer. Several life offices, indeed, set forth the advantage of accumulations of money in their hands compared with the interest received upon money deposited in banks. I have such a table before me contrasting the value of life policies with the benefits accruing from deposits of fixed sums in banks, and if this contrast can be applied to policies which run their course and become claims in the ordinary way, it can just as well apply to surrender values, provided the client is made to understand plainly the conditions under which the business is conducted, provided also the office issuing the policy is not occupied in accumulating dishonest profits. There is no advantage gained by concealing from those who take out life policies that it is an expensive method of saving money. At the very best it must be this, but the justification for taking out a policy lies in the fact that it is a provision against the unforeseen, and it ought to be made attractive to the community by the liberality with which people who insure are treated when they may be compelled by force of circumstances to abandon the contract.

I have looked into the offers of surrender value made by two eminent and wealthy Scotch life offices in respect to policies for £1,000 " with profits " that have been twenty-eight years in existence, and cannot say that I have found either of them satisfactory, but one is much more so than the other. At the rates of premium charged and left for accumulation, after allowing liberally for expenses—the net premiums, that is to say, as invested at 4 per cent. compound interest—the actual cash behind each of these policies ought to be at the end of the twenty-eight years about £1,000, more rather than less, especially more if the average interest earned has exceeded 4 per cent. Now one of these offices offers about £700 as surrender value upon the policy of £1,000 twenty-eight years old, and the other only £500. These amounts in each instance cover not merely the amount of the policy itself, but the surrender value of the accrued bonus as representing profits, and in one case the amount of such accrued bonuses credited to the policy exceeds £300. In other words, were the policy to become a claim at once, the office would have to pay between £1,300 and £1,400 upon it. It follows that the office which gives the better surrender value reserves at least £300, in the shape of money actually in hand, to cover the general risks of the business, and it may be that is not far from a fair proportion ; but the same cannot be said of the other office, which keeps full half of the actually accumulated money. Such conduct is little better than highway robbery, and I should never recommend anybody to take out a policy in that office.

Allowing for what is called the expenses "loading," the net sum in premiums paid over by the policy-holder in the course of these twenty-eight years should amount to between £590 and £620. This is after deducting a fairly high percentage for expenses, and the only inference I can draw is that the office which offers to return less than the amount it has received in net premiums, without counting any compound interest whatever, after paying all its expenses, is not treating its policy-holders with an approach to common fairness. One of the offices I am dealing with is proprietary and the other mutual, and it is the proprietary office which gives the worse surrender value; but the cause of the difference need not necessarily lie in the constitution of the office. It is much more likely to be, in regard to the more niggardly one, an inheritance from a bad past. It is an office which does not openly publish surrender values as its rival does, so that every policy issued by it which threatens to lapse is a matter of bargaining, and the spirit doubtless prevails of making the best possible for the office out of every failure. Probably enough, in the course of years, those policies which become claims in the ordinary way reap some benefit from this short-sightedness in the form of augmented bonuses, or the total of the funds in hand may be swollen out to an extent which gratifies vanity, and also opens the door to such impostures as the "natural premium" or "assessment" experiments already described; but the sharp practice is none the less objectionable on that account, and it ought to be abandoned.

In short, the action of one at least of these offices in this matter of surrender values is typical of a widely prevalent abuse which must be remedied if life insurance is to become really attractive, and those life offices which are the first to reform their practice towards the unfortunates who cannot continue to pay up will be sure to find their reward in augmented business. Everything is known to the conductors of the business, every risk except the risk of a world-wide credit catastrophe, and at any moment the actual cash value of a policy can be stated with extreme nicety. Consequently there ought to be no difficulty whatever in the way of a surrender value table being issued by every office doing life insurance business.

Defective though our home life insurance habits may be towards the unfortunates who fall out of the race, the worst of them are, one may say, princely in their liberality compared with the alien offices, some among whom do an imposing

amount of " new " business, business that seldom
lives to become old. These alien offices may be
said to live by robbing the poor, and some of
them do it with an affectation of liberality, not
to say pure benevolence, which serves but to add
to the disgust their maleficent industry excites.
All the more reason for avoiding their snares.

7. RATES OF INTEREST

Another matter of considerable importance to
those who wish to take out life policies centres in
the average rates of interest actually earned by
the office they go to, and the rate at which it
calculates its accumulations at compound interest.
The present generation has seen a great change
in the fructifying attributes of saved money.
Owing to a variety of influences, which need not
be described in detail, the rate of interest upon
such first-class securities as life offices are war-
ranted in purchasing has, until within the past
four years, materially and steadily declined, so
that while a generation ago it was easily possible
to get $4\frac{1}{2}$ and not difficult to get 5 per cent. as an
average upon invested money, it is now, and notwithstanding the recent decline in prices on the
Stock Exchange, difficult to get $3\frac{1}{2}$, and not pru-

dent to look for more than 4 per cent. This
change must obviously affect the value of with
profit policies, the rates of premium charged, and,
in extreme cases, even the stability of the office.
In order to understand the subject, it may be well
to advert here to what are called quinquennial or,
in some instances, septennial valuations. This is
an old practice amongst life offices, by which
they take elaborate and complete stock of their
positions every five or seven years. I have never
been able to see why there should be such long
intervals between balancings up, and think that
the practice now adopted by one or two offices of
annual balancings ought long ago to have become
the general usage. Be this as it may, the quinquennial valuation is, so far as the insured are
concerned, an opportunity to enable them to
judge whether the office is conducting its business
upon safe lines or otherwise. All that the candidate for insurance requires to look at is the rate
at which the actuarial valuer calculates the accumulation of the office's funds at compound interest.
Formerly actuaries were justified in relying upon
4 per cent., and making their forecast of compound
interest accumulations on that basis, whereas now
the most prudent and careful offices do not count

on more than 2½ per cent. It should be explained
that the quinquennial valuation relates to the
future quite as much as to the past, so far as
the policy-holder is concerned. The office, let us
suppose, has £2,000,000 invested and an annual
premium income of so much. During the expired
five years it has received an aggregate of so much
in premiums, and so much in interest, rents, and
dividends, and it has paid out so much in claims
and so much in expenses. The funds invested
have accumulated at such and such a rate, and
after meeting all claims there should be, if the
forecast of five years before was prudent, a certain
balance left over. If interest has been over-esti-
mated, or if the rate of mortality or of current
expenditure has exceeded expectations, or if unforeseen losses have occurred, there may be a
deficit.

That is all simple enough, but it is not sufficient
for the purpose in hand. The actuary proceeds
on the basis of these figures of the past experience to reckon what will be the course of business
in the coming five years, what the result to actual
members of the combination; and one of the main
elements in his calculation, apart from mortality
experience, the ratio of expenses to income, and

other purely actuarial matters, is the expected rate of interest at which the funds in hand and to be received will roll up. If the rate of interest assumed is a high one, the profits of the coming five years will probably look large and give a prospect of handsome future "bonuses" to those policy-holders who share in the "profits." If the rate is small, on the other hand, the accumulations will bulk much less pleasantly to the eye, and the bonuses may seem comparatively insignificant.

It might, however, happen, were a high rate of accumulation relied upon, that the end of the next quinquennium would find the office short of funds. Instead of a surplus there might be a deficiency, and according to the amount of that deficiency would be the danger and the disappointment. It is not by any means a rare experience for offices to fall into this disagreeable position. They may have been overtaken by a decline in the rate of interest, and may, perhaps, have been compelled also during the five years to meet a somewhat larger volume of claims than had been looked for, or they may have indulged too freely in outlays to secure new business, and the consequence is, when the accounts come to be made up, that there is no bonus available for

profit-sharing policies, or only such an insignificant one as will deprive the office of attractiveness.

The moral of all this is to avoid offices which
reckon to accumulate their funds at high rates of
interest, and to select those which at the outside
look for their funds to roll up at a compound
interest of no more than 3 per cent. Some of the
best offices now reckon their rates of accumulation
on what is called a $2\frac{1}{2}$ per cent. basis only, and
from the point of view of the policy-holder these
are the safest of all, other conditions being likewise good. Still, even this prudence may be
carried to excess, and has its drawbacks for the
heirs of those who die soon. It is seldom that
money earns so little as $2\frac{1}{2}$ per cent., but whatever
it yields beyond that figure goes, or should go,
to swell reserves and to augment long-distant
bonuses, bonuses accruing on policies that do not
become claims for many years, at the expense
of claims arising during the current quinquennium.
It is thus possible to be over-prudent in the matter
of interest rates, especially when these are fixed
excessively low for a long term of years ahead.
All the more ground, then, for urging an abandon-
ment of the five-yearly or seven-yearly system

of valuations or actuarial vaticinations. Let the business of the past year be vigilantly reviewed and its experience, added to that of former years and modified thereby, be utilised for the calculations relating to the current or coming year.

It may be, and often is, said by the mere uninstructed individual who comes from the mass of the public to insure his life that he is being cheated if the rate at which the money is accumulated is estimated too low. The profits upon his policy will not be so high as if a better rate of interest had been fixed upon, one more in accordance with the actual experiences of the office. "Why," it will be asked, "should an office, whose actual average interest and dividend earnings for the past five years was $3\frac{1}{2}$ or 4 per cent., calculate its accumulations for the coming five years at only $2\frac{1}{2}$? That looks like cheating the profit-sharing policy-holder of 1 per cent. of the accumulation upon his money."

Nothing of the kind may happen should a policy continue over several quinquennia. Upon such the actual earnings in excess of the forecast are, or should be, merely so much money to the good. The bonus that becomes payable as representing the policy-holder's share in the gains is in that event not improbably increased, will certainly be so if the office is honest. The bonus, in other words, is larger than the holder of the policy had been led to expect, and he is gratified by seeing a bigger addition to the capital value of his policy, or a larger sum available to meet reductions in premiums, than he had been told to look for. All that the fine rate of interest means for policies which survive the quinquennium is that the office is trading cautiously and not throwing out extravagantly dressed-up baits in order to induce people to insure. It is running no risks, and consequently its clients are protected. But policies becoming claims within the quinquennium may very well suffer. There is really no reason, except that found in old usage, for continuing this habit.

There is another point which demands an intelligent appreciation on the part of the public. Quite a number of offices in this country, especially those of colonial or foreign origin, deliberately trade upon chances of accumulating funds at a rate of interest considerably higher than those deemed safe or proved by experience to be safe in the United Kingdom. I have no doubt whatever that the offices which conduct their business on these lines will disappoint their clients. They offer more than they can pay either now or in the future. Such offices are not exempt from the tendency to shrink which has affected all rates of interest during the present generation, a tendency that is universal and probably permanent, in spite of accidental interruptions, such as the occurrence of a costly war or some other wealth-exhausting calamity. It is the invariable experience of a new country undergoing settlement that capital is most expensive when the country is young. Rates of interest may range from 8 to 10 or 12 per cent. in newly occupied territories, because money therein is invariably scarce. Capital has to be imported, and is lent upon securities of untried and unknown value, therefore it is both scarce and dear. As a country progresses, however, and begins to accumulate capital of its own, the rates of interest invariably tend downwards.

That has been the experience in all our white colonies and in the United States, and it is also the experience in South America. As capital accumulates, wealth in the hands of bankers, etc., grows in volume, and the rates of interest it can command tend to come down. Therefore a life office which conducts its business upon the assumption that high rates of interest will be permanent, and which enters into long contracts founded on this assumption, is certain, no matter what the push and go exhibited in conducting the business may be, to land its clients in losses. It either pays away too much on actual claims or promises too much in the future, and affliction for all concerned follows. Sooner or later that must be the case with many alien offices, and therefore I insist the more that those who are about to insure their lives should carefully examine into the record of the offices whose prospectuses they may study in regard to the rates adopted by them in calculating the speed at which the money in their hands will accumulate at compound interest. Far better go to a $2\frac{1}{2}$ per cent. office than to a 4 per cent. one.

8. RISKS ATTENDING ENDOWMENT INSURANCE

Probably the system of insurance called endowment will first bring to light the delusive character of promises made by life offices that habitually disregard prudence in the matter of the rate of interest they assume in calculating prospective profits. These endowment policies fall due at fixed dates, and if an office, relying upon a

H

steady income from interest at the rate of 5 per cent., makes promises of bonus and profit additions at the end of the term calculated upon this rate of interest, or something near it, there is certain to be disappointment, especially when excessive current expenditure is likewise indulged in and excused by the same assumption. Already many sorrowful results have come painfully home to British investors in endowment policies sold by alien offices, and they are now aware of the deception thus, perhaps involuntarily, certainly unscrupulously, practised upon them. There is far less of this kind of deception practised by British offices than by alien ones. Nevertheless, some of our own life offices are much too heedless in disregarding the tendency of interest to decline, and continue to adopt high rates of interest in dealing with anticipations of the future. These offices are thus preparing for themselves and for their clients bitter disillusionment, and they ought to be avoided by every prudent citizen who desires to make a solid provision against the risks of the unknown.

9. BONUSES USED TO MEET PREMIUMS

What has been said above about surrender values has been based upon the tacit assumption that there is no alternative offered to a holder of a life policy other than its surrender, should he be unable to continue the payment of the premiums on the scale originally contracted for. This, however, is by no means the fact, and hence the practical value of taking out policies endowed with a share in what is called the profits. Let us suppose that a man has paid the premiums steadily upon his life policy of £1,000 over a period of twenty years, and has never touched any of the bonuses assigned at each valuation as profit upon that policy. He will in this way, after a term of years, have a fund over and above the nominal amount of the insurance which may amount to £300, or to £400 in the case of a first-class office, upon which he can draw in order to tide over a period of distress, and still leave the original sum fixed in the policy untouched. The office will be quite willing to devote this bonus money to the payment of premiums during the time the policy-holder may be unable himself to find the money, or it will pay whatever proportion of such premiums he is unable to meet out of this accumulated fund. Should that fund, through lapse of years, have become large, the money may be sufficient to meet all further payments upon the policy, helped as it will be by future profit accumulations. In short, there are a great number of devices which may be fallen upon, given the accumulation of bonuses, in order to protect the policy-holder from loss. No reputable office now cancels a policy through accidental failure to meet premiums when due, and I do not think any office refuses to employ the accumulated bonuses, or the cash equivalent thereof, which, however, is a very different thing, in paying premiums in order to keep policies alive.

Some offices take other methods of easing payments for their clients. They begin by charging a tolerably high scale of premium for a fixed term of years. At the end of that period, if the policy is still in force, a reduction in the premium takes place, the office automatically applying the accrued profits, or part of them, to meet the recurring obligation. One old and important office, for example, charges a fixed premium for the first seven years on a tolerably high scale, and then applies the profits that have accrued to the life policy in effecting an immediate reduction of 55 per cent. in the future premiums. Other offices also have a gradually descending scale which would ultimately wipe the premium payments out should the policy-holder live long.

Then, again, almost every office will allow an agreed upon proportion of the annual premiums to stand over and accumulate against the capital of a policy as a debt. This, however, is an expensive method of surmounting hard times, because the rule is to charge 5 per cent. interest upon such advances, and were the plan resorted to early in the life of a policy, it would probably be cheaper for the holder to get the old contract cancelled and enter into a new one on a basis more within his present means.

One advantage of a life policy, after it has been in existence for a sufficient number of years to become a pawnable security, is that money can be raised upon it in an emergency, and nearly all reputable life offices are willing to make advances upon their own policies to an amount inside their surrender value, whatever that may be. Generally speaking, they charge 5 per cent. for such advances, so that the borrowing cannot be considered too cheap, and, possibly enough, those in need of temporary aid of this description might sometimes be able to get the money on the security of their policy at a lower rate elsewhere ; but it is not for the good of policy-holders that borrowing should be easy upon their contracts, and I certainly do not recommend any ordinary householder to take out a life policy merely as an instrument for raising credit. There may, however, arise occasions when it would be expedient, or even necessary, to take out a policy as collateral security for advances of money required in a man's business ; and no small part of the policies issued by some offices is of this description.

Such policies, however, come within the special category with which I hardly think it necessary to deal, and very often they are taken out for a fixed short term of years, either to protect those who make advances in some trading enterprise or for other purposes of a like kind. An enormous number of policies issued by the United States life offices appear to be of this transitory description. A man, let us suppose, has to give a guarantee against loss to those assisting him in some enterprise into which he has entered, and a policy representing a laying of odds against death for one or more years is the readiest form under which this guarantee can be provided.   Betting business of this sort is usually extremely profitable to the offices conducting it, and helps to enable them to spend money on a scale of reckless profusion which our old-fashioned carefully managed British offices dare not launch into.   But then our offices really insure life.

10. PAID-UP POLICIES TAKEN IN EXCHANGE

Nearly all life insurance offices nowadays grant paid-up policies for smaller amounts than the sum originally insured in the event of holders becoming unable to continue premium payments, and some of them publish regularly tables exhibiting the amount of such paid-up policies at all ages of a policy.   This practice represents a great reform, and the terms offered are generally fair.   Often the amount of the new policy is equal to, and occasionally it exceeds, that of the old.   All depends upon the ages of the policy given up and of the person insured.   A man of seventy, for example, whose policy has been forty years in force, has ceased to be a "risk," in any substantial sense, to a well-conducted office, and the most that should be deducted from the contract of such a one's policy and bonuses ought to be little, if anything, more than some small sum representing his share in the current expenditure for the few years remaining as his average expectation of life. It is otherwise with a young man, aged say thirty-five, whose policy has been but ten years in force. Should the ability of such a man to provide the annual premiums cease, he may be reasonably thankful if the office he is in gives him a paid-up policy of £500 to £600 in lieu of the £1,000 with profits originally contracted for. But all particulars of this kind ought to be known and understood beforehand, and it is the duty of every candidate for life insurance, no matter in what form, to make himself acquainted with all the facts.

II. PROOF OF AGE

On one point let every insurant be most vigilant —the proof of age. Before paying the first premium the candidate should demand an acknowledgment from the office that the evidence of date of birth tendered by him has been accepted, and that acknowledgment should really be endorsed upon every policy ; but habits are still lax in this direction, and the heirs of many old people born before the days of compulsory registration have often to endure much vexation before claims are admitted, all because birth evidence is not forthcoming in due form. Some offices not only make the absence of such evidence a pretext for delaying payment of claims, but for deductions from the amounts for which they are liable. Practices of this sort are both disreputable and dishonest, and we should stamp them out by ruling the acceptance of a given premium to be proof that the policy-holder's statement of age was accepted as correct at the time the contract was entered into. Until that reform is accomplished, candidates for life insurance must by their vigilance at the outset protect those who come after them. And the production of a copy of the birth certificate is now a matter of no difficulty; should the candidate for insurance possess no document of the kind, it can always be obtained from the Registrars General in London, Edinburgh, or Dublin, on payment of a small fee, and once provided it should be attached to the policy, so as to be available at once when the policy becomes a claim.

12. ALL THE SHAPES A POLICY MAY ASSUME

Doubtful as to my ability to set forth all the facts, I applied to a distinguished actuary, a friend of mine, to summarise for me the varieties of ways related to life and its affairs in which one could insure, and will now proceed to set forth the information he kindly put together for me. It gathers much of what has been already said, as it were, into a focus.

First as to premiums. These may be paid either annually, half-yearly, quarterly, or monthly, according to the desire or circumstances of the candidate for insurance ; or finally, if the policy is terminated at a fixed date, the whole amount may be paid down at once and the transaction completed for good and all. This last form of payment merely represents an investment at compound interest, or should do that, and the investor in such cases should see to it that, at least, the whole of his capital is returnable to him at any time after a year.

Premium payments further may be eased by various systems, several of which have been already mentioned. Some offices provide that only half the premium is payable for the first five years, the other half accumulating against the policy as a debt bearing interest. It need hardly be said that this method of insuring should as much as possible be avoided. It implies a grasping of too much on the part of the person taking out a policy. Far better insure for a smaller sum within present means, and as one grows richer take out other policies. This form of premium is called the half-credit system, and there is another form somewhat similar to it called the renewal term assurance. In this instance a low premium is paid for a term of years, and thereafter the full premium at the proposer's age is charged right up to the end of the term, or the life, as the case may be. Finally the premiums may be reduced by discounting future bonuses, if it be a with profit policy that is purchased. Sometimes these bonuses have accumulated for a number of years, and may be almost, or quite, sufficient to relieve the policy-holder of further liability for the remainder of the term of his policy or of his life. These discountings may take various forms, such as insuring at prime cost or cost price, or by discounting the bonus, or by a minimum scale of premiums, but on the whole the simplest form of life insurance remains the best for the bulk of those who seek to protect dependants from disaster by this method of investment.

Having dealt with the premiums, it is now expedient to indicate the variety of policies which can be taken out. There is, to begin with, the life policy, where the sum assured is payable at death. This may take two forms, either with profits or without. It is more in accordance with the habits of the human mind to take with profit policies, but these are by no means necessary, and for people of small means might not always be the best. Each man must decide for himself. Along with these we place the various kinds of endowment policies, the amount insured being payable at a specified age or at death, should death take place before the expiry of the term. These policies assume various forms. They may be double-endowment assurance, where double the amount assured is paid if the policy-holder survives the stipulated age, or a semi-endowment assurance, where half the amount assured is paid if the policy-holder dies before the stipulated age. Then there are settlement endowment policies, upon which the sum assured is payable on the death of the last survivor, say husband or wife, combined with deferred insurance to the husband on his attainment of an agreed age, or to the wife on her husband's death. Complicated though these policies look, they are all effected on well-understood lines, and show that life offices have to meet clients in every conceivable position. Then there are policies on which the sum stipulated becomes payable only in the event of death within the specified time. These are called term assurances. A man pays a small premium for a policy entitling his heirs to the receipt of a more or less important sum should he die within a year. If the term is longer, the premium will be higher. Another form of this policy is sometimes called indemnity insurance, where the sum stipulated becomes payable only in the event of death before a specified age. Finally there is joint life assurance, where the amount insured becomes payable on the extinction of two lives, and one form of this is called a convertible partnership policy, which means that in the event of the joint policy being no longer required through the death of one or more of the participants therein, a separate policy will be granted to each surviving partner at the rate of premium chargeable at the original date of the contract.

Many other varieties of policies, all relating to human life in some form or other, can be acquired, and amongst these may be enumerated estate duty policies, under which the whole or part of the sum stipulated in the policy is payable to the Commissioners of Inland Revenue for death duties upon the insurant's estate. Settlement

policies are another form of insurance, which can
be taken out under the Married Women's Property
Act, and most offices, if required to do so, will
now issue non-forfeitable policies, the distinguish-
able quality of which is the protection of the
insured against loss in the event of a failure to
continue premiums. Under this contract a policy
for a certain proportion of the sum originally
insured is at once granted. This scheme is generally applied to limited premium policies. Guarantee policies constitute another form of insurance,
which is in the nature both of an investment and
of a protection to heirs against premature death.
Instead of handing over the money insured by
the policy at death of the person insured, so much
per cent. is allowed upon its amount to the heirs
for a fixed number of years after death. In fact,
an annuity is paid for a certain number of years,
and at the end of the time [the capital sum is
handed over. One other form may be mentioned,
called the reversible premium policy. Here the
sum insured is payable only at death, but premiums cease at a specified age, and after that the
office returns one premium each year as long as
the person in whose favour the policy was taken
out continues to live. These are all ingenious

ways of tempting people to make provision for the unknown future, and every one of them has something to commend it, while some of them are distinctly advantageous, as embodying at one and the same time a provision for those who come after the policy-holder and a help to said policy-holder in the closing years of life. Given a people habituated to thrift and forethought, and an unlimited field for investment, and the "old age pensions" difficulty might at once be solved for everybody as no politician could ever solve it. Thrift alone, however, is helpless, because no territory provides scope for investments at interest commensurate with the old age wants of its entire population. Hence but a limited number can provide themselves with the means of comfort in declining years, drawn from invested money. It follows that universal old age pensions can only be furnished by an annual levy or rate.

CHAPTER VI

MARINE INSURANCE AND THE CORPORATION OF LLOYD'S

ALTHOUGH the main subject of this little book is life insurance, it will not be without interest to glance at some of the other varieties of business having for object the protection of individuals against loss in the enterprises undertaken by them. All forms of insurance are based upon the same principle of averages which is especially the characteristic of life insurance, but the data upon which insurance business other than life is conducted are, as a rule, less scientific, and the risks run always of a quite different class.

Of all forms of insurance, marine is the oldest. It is disputed whether the practice of insuring the risks of shipowners and owners of ships' cargoes began in the fifteenth or the sixteenth century, but there seems good evidence that the custom was known in Catalonia in the early part of the fifteenth century, and some go so far as to assert that it was known to the Phœnicians. Unfortunately the records of Carthage and Tyre have been so completely lost that there is no means of verifying a conjecture of this description. Others again tell us that the Romans practised marine insurance, but the only proofs cited in support of this statement are that the Government of Rome during the second Punic War undertook to indemnify those contractors employed in transporting ammunition and provisions to Spain against loss by the enemy or from storms, and the Emperor Claudius is likewise stated to have entered into some contract with the shippers of corn from Africa to relieve the scarcity in the city. Out of this last guarantee a trade is alleged to have arisen similar to that known as " coffin" ships in the oversea traffic of modern England, whereby sham or inferior cargoes and rotten ships were over-insured in order to make a fraudulent profit out of the freight lost at sea. Shipwrecks were reported which never in any honest or straightforward manner took place, and when shattered vessels were freighted with articles of little value for the purpose of being sunk, the crews sometimes escaped in boats, but more often were drowned, on the good

I

old principle embodied in the saying, " Dead men tell no tales." The unity of human nature would thus appear to be established, but it cannot be considered that either of these examples proves the habit of insurance against losses at sea to have prevailed amongst the merchants of the Roman Empire. The contrary inference seems the natural one, else why was it necessary for the Government to step in and undertake the risks, throwing upon the nation losses that in the modern world are borne by private individuals or joint-stock companies?

A recent French writer, however, M. Thomereau, in an article contributed by him to the *Dictionnaire du Commerce*, edited by Messrs. Yves Guyot and A. Raffalovich, points out that although there is no trace of anything resembling modern marine insurance in the history of Egypt, Greece, or Rome, there did obtain almost from time immemorial a sort of mutual insurance or clubbing of interests in the conduct of the sea traffic of ancient nations. He calls it the custom of *avaries communes*, and the word *avaries* may be translated as port dues. It came into the French through the Italian, and implies both ordinary port charges and a rate levied to meet extraordinary expenses, such as

damages through loss or injury to ships and cargoes
during the voyage, or injury to merchandise stored
until it could be shipped. M. Thomereau says that
this form of mutual insurance was practised both
by the Phœnicians and the Romans. He further
holds that as early as the middle of the eleventh
century mutual support in affliction of this description took a form that approaches that of modern
marine insurance as we know it, and he cites a
statute of the town of Trani, on the Adriatic, dated
1063. That was a period of barbarism, when the
ocean was scoured by pirates, and in order to protect the merchants, ships were gathered together
so as to form a sort of sea caravan, sailing in company for mutual protection, and ready to fight in
common should they be attacked. The contract
was to the effect that the damages suffered through
the pirates by any one ship in the fleet, or by any
cargo, would be made good by the owners of those
that had escaped.

Anyway, marine insurance is the oldest form of
this business of dividing risks so as to minimise
losses, now familiar the world over, and, as we have
said, the principle governing this business is precisely the same as that affecting life insurance,
except that there is no question of accumulating

capital at compound interest, or anything of that sort. The risk underwritten by those who insure ships and their cargoes is limited to the voyage, but the premium charged is determined by the experience of a long series of years, by the character of the ships upon which policies are underwritten, and the nature of the cargo. Hence we see vessels classed in Lloyd's Register according to their age and seaworthiness, and the premium charged differs according to the class into which the vessel is placed, as well as according to the nature of its cargo. The rates of premium on a first-class ocean liner, carrying selected cargo and rarely wrecked should be, and is, less than that upon a vessel, no matter however seaworthy, carrying petroleum, or coal, or other cargo liable to catch fire by spontaneous combustion, or otherwise inflammable. The seas traded in and the seasons of the year must also be taken into account, and a variety of other circumstances which need not be set forth here in detail.

Suppose a vessel is worth £100,000 and that it carries a safe cargo of an equal value, and further that the experience of the underwriters in this class of vessel and branch of commerce indicates that only one in a hundred of these vessels is on the average lost, the whole £200,000 involved in this case ought to be insured for little more than 1 per cent. or £2,000, or say, allowing for expenses, commissions and so on, £2,500. When such a contract is entered into the policy for the gross amount is split up into small fragments, and each underwriter, whether a joint-stock insurance company or an individual member of the Corporation of Underwriters in Lloyd's, puts down his name for the amount he is willing to stake as his share in the guarantee, and receives the proportionate share in the stipulated premium. In some instances the premium might be 2 per cent., in others 5 per cent., but always the risk is divided up in this manner, so that no individual guarantor need take an excessive risk in any one adventure. When the voyage is over the risk is ended, and the premium, less commissions, is the underwriters' profit. If the cargo or a portion of it has been seriously damaged, it does not follow that the underwriters are liable, unless the damage exceeds 3 per cent. of the value of the goods injured.

When, however, something goes wrong, a traffic immediately springs up in the fragments of a marine policy. Supposing the ship is overdue for a length of time which excites alarm, the underwriters immediately set to work to endeavour to transfer their risks, fearing total loss. A man who stands to lose £2,000 if the vessel is a complete wreck proceeds to transfer his risk by offering a higher premium to somebody else to take it. He may be willing to sacrifice 10, 15, 20, 50, and in some cases 80 or more per cent. of his share in the policy, rather than encounter the loss of the entire sum. Hence we are continually hearing, or reading in the newspapers, of the premium on such and such a ship, long overdue, advancing in the manner just indicated. One buyer sells to another who hopes that the news of the safe arrival of the ship will immediately come in. Delay continues, and this purchaser in turn takes alarm and sells to somebody else willing to take the chance for a tempting sum down. It thus generally happens that if the vessel does ultimately prove to be lost, the money staked upon it has to be found by such a number of people that the individual suffering is small. Each grade of sellers at the advancing premium diminishes its portion of the loss, and the man who has underwritten £1,000 at, say, 1¼ per cent. may be the smallest loser of all. On the other hand, should the vessel ultimately arrive, the profit on the transaction may be in like manner so

dispersed that the ultimate holders of the underwriters' fragments of the policy may make very
little profit, while those who had sold in fear
necessarily make no profit at all.   For clearly if a
man who has underwritten a policy at a minute
rate of premium sacrifices perhaps twice or three
times the sum he received in order to rid himself
of his risk, he loses the difference between what he
pays and what he received, whether the vessel
comes safely to harbour or not.

It will thus be seen that the business of marine
insurance contains highly speculative elements
fascinating to many minds, but also occasionally
involving intense anxiety to those who have
entered into the contract of indemnity.   Yet on
the average, and in the long-run, the business of
marine insurance is clearly a safe and profitable
one, as the records of our joint-stock marine insurance companies prove.   They have all accumulated more or less massive reserves, so that even
in bad years none but the most recklessly managed,
or the temporarily unfortunate in an exceptional
degree, realise a loss on the entire business done
during the twelve months.   Their risks often run
into millions of pounds during that time, and
sometimes a long season of misfortune will over-

take those engaged in the business—a year of unusual storms, a run of disastrous accidents—so that the profits made almost disappear ; but yet on the average the business is good and safe, because long experience has taught those engaged in it to measure their risks with a sufficient amount of exactitude to protect them from permanent injury.

Not only is marine insurance the oldest form of providing against risks of loss from causes beyond the foresight or control of those engaged in commerce, but it is also in many ways the most picturesque and interesting. Were I competent, a volume of much romantic fascination might be written, giving the story of the development of this form of insurance at home and abroad. Naturally it has attained its highest efficiency in the United Kingdom, which possesses the greatest mercantile marine the world ever saw, a marine that conducts even now, and in spite of all com- petitors, almost half the ocean commerce of the world. But the business of our marine insurance offices is by no means confined to ships sailing under the British flag. They have ramifications the world over, and through foreign marine insurance offices located in London, Liverpool, Glasgow, or other parts of the United Kingdom, the capital of the English marine offices and of Lloyd's Corporation—the centre of them all, though not the dominant power—is deeply interested in the shipping of foreign nations.

Mention of Lloyd's compels some notice of the picturesque and fascinating side of this branch of insurance business. The name is known the world over in two capacities, which must not be confounded. Lloyd's proper is a corporation, at least it has been a corporation since 1871, formed by men whose primary business it was and is to insure risks on sea-going ships, but it has developed into something unique in the world as a centre of insurance business of all kinds. We shall return to that aspect presently. All that it is necessary now to state is that the name Lloyd's comes from the keeper of a coffee-house in the seventeenth century named Edward Lloyd, at whose place of business the early professional insurers of shipping risks met. In 1692 this man removed his coffee-house from Tower Street to Lombard Street, and in 1774 the association of underwriters of shipping risks which had gathered in the coffee-house was moved to a portion of the Royal Exchange formerly occupied by the East India Company. During the long revolutionary and Napoleonic wars this association of underwriters, which still .stuck to the original coffee-house name, rose to great importance and wealth. Partly by reason of the necessity over-sea traders were under of doing their best to protect themselves against war losses, high premiums ruled, and the risks proving on the average less than had been anticipated, enormous fortunes accrued to not a few.

Since then Lloyd's as a centre of marine insurance has developed in wealth and influence, notwithstanding keen competition from outside. So great has this competition become through the existence of powerfully wealthy and excellently managed marine insurance companies, in London and Liverpool especially, and in some foreign countries also, that Lloyd's has in great measure ceased to dominate the marine insurance business, and has found scope for its energies in many other directions. It none the less remains the greatest centre of information about shipping in the world —a unique institution. As Mr. Douglas Owen said in his admirable lecture on Marine Insurance, delivered at the Salters' Hall, St. Swithin's Lane, on December 17th, 1902 :—

" Lloyd's is the centre of a sort of spider's web of shipping news. The filaments of the web have their attachment in all the ports of the world. Not a ship can arrive or leave or a casualty be known but immediately a thread to the central and sleepless brain is set vibrating with the news, which is immediately posted up on the board at Lloyd's and distributed generally. In this respect Lloyd's has no competitor. It stands practically alone in its glory, the pride of every Englishman, the object of the respectful admiration of every foreigner. And when at a leading foreign port a vacancy occurs in the appointment of Lloyd's Agent, the best and most respected firms at the port keenly compete for the honour of the appointment. Any man who, like myself, has the privilege to serve on Lloyd's Agency Committee will tell you so."

Returning to the business done at Lloyd's, it is necessary first of all to distinguish the corporation of underwriters bearing this name from the institution called Lloyd's Register. The latter has nothing to do with the former, being merely a voluntary association of members of the shipping community, whose primary business it is to classify vessels according to their quality as carriers or as seaworthy vessels. This society has ramifications the world over, but, as Mr. Douglas Owen points out, the agents of Lloyd's Corporation of Under-

writers must not be confounded with Lloyd's
Register surveyors. They are two distinct bodies
of men, obeying authorities entirely independent
of each other. It is thanks to the Register that
the business community of this country has a
complete catalogue of the mercantile marines of
the world, with the condition of every vessel
therein briefly and distinctly indicated. You often
hear the expression, "A1 at Lloyd's," which means
that the vessel thus marked by the authorities
of Lloyd's Register is in the very first rank as a
sea-going ship.

Lloyd's Corporation of Underwriters, on the
other hand, is an association of men engaged in
the business of insurance. Primarily this business
was marine insurance and fire insurance so far as
it related to shipping business. Fires at docks
and storage yards, for instance, would come
within the legitimate range of the Lloyd's
Corporation. Owing, however, to the competition of the powerful companies already mentioned,
the underwriters at Lloyd's have been driven into
a variety of lines of business not at all contemplated by their progenitors, but perfectly within
their rights as members of the incorporation.
For Lloyd's resembles the Stock Exchange in

this, that just as stockbrokers and jobbers may buy and sell what they please, so its members are free to do any kind of insurance business so long as they do it honestly and " on the square." All the corporation does is to demand certain guarantees for honourable dealing and for fulfilment of contracts on the part of its members. Thus each man who becomes a member of Lloyd's has to deposit securities with the committee of management to protect clients from loss. In all other respects, however, he is free to do as he pleases, and the consequence is that Lloyd's is not merely a centre of shipping information, but a place where almost every conceivable unforeseen contingency can be provided against by the payment of a premium. Epidemic diseases, for instance, can always be insured against by individuals at Lloyd's. Whenever a small-pox epidemic arises, business there becomes brisk in policies under which certain payments are guaranteed should the purchaser catch the disease. Numbers of people go and pay premiums to the underwriters covering certain sums in the event of an attack. The latest of these diseases added to the list is appendicitis. Underwriters at Lloyd's will insure anyone against the outlay involved in an operation for this terrifying affliction.

Occasionally, also, policies can be taken out at Lloyd's insuring against the expenses of twins, and one of the common risks accepted there may be described as "sporting," such as the loss involved by the stoppage of cricket or football matches or race meetings by frost or snow. Processions, again, and the letting of seats in connection therewith, can be insured at Lloyd's, so that those who speculate in the erection of seated stages can get their loss partially or wholly made good in the event of the seats finding no sufficient number of paying occupants. In matters of fisc, too, merchants can go to Lloyd's and insure against a change of taxation in the coming budget. Supposing the fear exists that fresh taxation is to be imposed on tea, or sugar, or wheat, the trader can go to Lloyd's and obtain a guarantee that any loss, up to a maximum amount specified, he thinks himself liable to incur through this change will be made good. In like manner, if the fear prevails that taxes are to be removed, leading to a fall in prices, the resulting or probable loss upon stocks in hand can be provided against by a policy at Lloyd's. You can hardly imagine a contingency in the complex life of modern society that the underwriters there, one or other of them or groups of them, are not willing to underwrite or guarantee. All you have to do is to find a broker skilled in the ways of the place and in the characters of the men doing business there, and put the matter into his hands. Lloyd's, for example, insured loans made to the Humberts on the faith of the contents of that mysterious safe, lately found empty. Valuable possessions, too, can be specially insured there, such as violins or pictures, works of art of any description ; and tourists can insure against the risks of particular journeys or voyages. Collectors can take out policies insuring them against the loss of their collections or valuables of any description ; holders of exhibitions can guarantee themselves against losses through the failure of the public to attend ; and one of the commonest lines of business done at Lloyd's is insurance against war risks during times of political excitement. Out of this business alone the underwriters there sometimes make magnificent profits.

If a church or dissenting chapel holds an annual bazaar or other fête at which money is collected, it can obtain at Lloyd's a guarantee that the result will not fall below the average. You can insure against death before a certain date for any sum necessary to cover liabilities on contracts undertaken, or any contingency whatsoever. Losses arising from burst pipes after frost can be insured against, and policies against accidents of all kinds can be taken out. Holders of football, golf, or other trophy cups, held for one year by the winner at his own risk, can be insured against loss by theft or otherwise ; and tradesmen can insure themselves against loss of profit arising, say, through the death of a member of the Royal Family, which would render coloured goods, silks, etc., for the time being valueless. Much of the business done is perhaps of the nature of simple betting, the purest gamble it might be called ; but it is legitimate enough, full of picturesque variety, and undoubtedly on the average profitable. What amount of risks may be carried at Lloyd's at any one time it is impossible to say, but the average nowadays is probably not much under £500,000,000, and the security deposited with the committee of Lloyd's Corporation may amount to about 1 per cent. of these risks. The mere statement of such figures, coupled with the fact that rarely if ever does any member of Lloyd's become a defaulter, shows how profitable on the average the business must be. One of the commonest forms of policy taken out when tariff changes are contemplated is really a kind of marine policy; that is to say, a "date of arrival" policy. Supposing new or enhanced duties are to come into force in the United States, or in some of our colonies, on the 1st of January next, policies can be taken out insuring the specified ship and cargo to arrive before the new duties are actually leviable. That means to say, if the ship does not reach port in time for its cargo to escape the additional taxation, the difference between the old duties and the new is made good to the shippers by the underwriters.

A brief sketch of this kind, for the materials of which I am indebted to Mr. Douglas Owen, will serve to indicate what a marvellous focus of business life and activity Lloyd's is. It is no longer a mere centre of marine insurance, although that is still the dominant characteristic of its business. All the great marine insurance companies around it, whose business in their particular line is in the aggregate far greater than anything that members of Lloyd's, merely as such, carry on, whether in their individual or in a collective capacity, must have their representatives in its underwriters' room, and its help is continually necessary in the conduct

K

of their business. In the lecture already quoted, Mr. Owen holds up to ridicule the antiquated form of the marine policy. It dates from somewhere in the middle of last century, and is adapted to modern ways by all sorts of additional clauses pasted on or written in, so that the result is often a document full of excellent value for the lawyers. But although the policy form may be antiquated, the actual business of marine insurance has attained the highest scientific development, and no words can be too strong in praise of the admirable system by which risks are handled and subdivided, losses adjusted and paid without the slightest hitch. The work involved is sometimes enormous, and a special class of loss assessors, called "average adjusters," are continually engaged in the business of making up the amount of the damage suffered ; but everything goes smoothly, and so wealthy and strong are the companies and individuals engaged in the business of marine insurance, that there is never any hitch in payments. The heaviest losses are met without a murmur, thanks in part to the minuteness of their subdivision, and there is on the whole no more valuable source of profit to a large class of British capitalists than marine insurance and its corollaries.

CHAPTER VII

FIRE AND MISCELLANEOUS INSURANCE

ANOTHER important branch of business which has risen to great proportions in modern times is insurance against fire, and perhaps the most interesting thing about this business is the tendency the statistics collected about it reveal for fires to increase in number and disastrousness when the business of any country is bad. From this it is to be guessed that human nature is not on the average greatly advanced in morality, for the inference must be that when fires multiply in this fashion, the increase cannot all be due to accident. It results, moreover, from this invariable rule that the cost of insurance against fire has to be increased to an extent that punishes the honest portion of the community, undoubtedly the great majority, In fire insurance, contracts are only for one year, just as in marine insurance

much of the liability is limited to the single
voyage, so that there is no necessity for the
elaborate calculations required in life insurance
business. All, practically, that the conductors of
fire insurance offices require to know is the
average number of fires in a given number of
houses within one twelvemonth. But this business
also has many ramifications, some of them of a
highly speculative kind, because there is such a
continual variety in the uses to which buildings
are put and in the nature of their contents.
Private dwellings in towns, for example, at any
rate in this country where they are mostly built
of brick or stone, rarely catch fire. I have been
told by an experienced fire insurance manager that
if the business the fire offices did were confined to
such private houses alone, 6d. per cent. per annum
would be a quite sufficient premium to cover all
risks. There are, however, an indefinite number
of businesses conducted in buildings that involve
much greater risks, as well as a few industries of
an inflammable kind, and I fear it has to be said
that the owners and tenants of private houses who
insure their buildings and furniture are charged
from 1s. 6d. to 2s. per cent. for the insurance of
fixed sums upon their property in the event of fire

destroying it, just because the risks of loss in these other and more dangerous directions are so great and so continually varying that the fire offices are compelled to protect themselves somehow. Without this backbone of insurance revenue from the private householder, it is probable that we should either have periodical crises in fire insurance, or that the premiums charged on many factories and warehouses would be prohibitory, and there have been several occasions within the present generation when catastrophes have occurred by which this class of insurance business has almost been brought to a standstill. The most notorious of these were the two burnings down of the city of Chicago, and in London we have had fires in Tooley Street, Cripplegate, and Wood Street, the last named being the home of most of our dry goods warehouses. These fires involved enormous losses to the insurance offices. The Tooley Street fire burnt for weeks.

In consequence of these and many other similar losses, premiums have been put up on various classes of business premises all over the country, and one of the products of such enhancement has been sullen discontent amongst the business people compelled to pay the revised premiums. Because of this discontent, we frequently see an attempt made to establish a new fire insurance company which shall conduct business on rates less onerous. It is almost impossible to build up a new fire insurance business in these days, yet we frequently see prospectuses of new fire offices launched in London or in provincial districts to undertake certain lines of business assumed to be too severely assessed in premiums by the existing offices. The attempt, however, almost invariably fails, and for one very simple reason. The new office which undertakes to accept risks upon inflammable kinds of property at lower rates than the old offices is compelled to carry the whole risks by itself, whereas the " tariff offices," as they are called—that is to say, the old-established offices—which all work together on an agreed upon scale of charges, inter-divide their risks. Suppose one office sells a policy involving a risk of £500,000 upon some great warehouse or factory, it does not keep the whole of this £500,000 to itself, but goes around and sub-insures with its neighbours, so that perhaps in the end it only retains an odd £50,000, or half that, as its particular risk. The mere fact, however, that these offices work together upon an agreed, perhaps identical, scale of charges shuts the door of the

new office which undercuts, and it is severely let
alone to face the whole loss, should any bad fire
occur amongst the properties insured by it.   Such
losses unfortunately often happen, and even when
they can get together a certain amount of business,
new fire offices nearly always either succumb or
are compelled to "enter the ring" in order to escape
destruction.   They cannot live alone.

I believe great reforms are required in the
management of fire business, and sympathise
strongly with those who struggle to escape from
the tyranny of the existing combination, a combination quite as thorough as any American trust
could be, but I am satisfied that the reforms are
not to be brought about by these attempts to
establish new rival offices professing to do business
on terms more favourable to the insurers.   I have
hopes that the offices themselves will see reason
for changing their system in some respects, and
there is one obvious direction in which they ought
to be able to do so with no difficulty, that is, in the
scale of their working charges.   I do not think one
amongst these offices conducts its business at a
lower rate than one-third of the premium income,
and many of them take from 35 to 40 per cent. of
that income to pay working expenses and com-

missions. This is a scale of extravagance which ought to be entirely unnecessary now that the business has been consolidated, and that all the offices work under practically the same tariff. It would take me far, however, to enter into this grievance in detail, and I merely mention the fact as one well worthy of consideration by the shareholders in our fire offices, and by the merchants and private citizens who insure.

Difficult though it may be to start and maintain a new fire insurance company on general lines, there yet exist a fair number of small companies that do a special kind of business. Altogether some sixty different organisations carry on fire insurance of one form or another in the United Kingdom, and an important proportion of these devote their organisations and means to special lines, such as the insurance of marine fires, of property connected with the cotton industry, and of ecclesiastical property. Some of the offices are purely local in their field of operations, as well as confined to special lines. About a score of insurance offices carry on life insurance as well as fire, often to the substantial benefit of the holders of life policies, and the number of important fire offices possessed of large funds does not much exceed two dozen. The accounts of twenty-five of them are analysed once a year in the *Investors' Review*, and according to the latest of these summaries, the funds accumulated by them over and above the amount of their paid-up capital on 31st December, 1902, exceeded £28,000,000. It is improbable that the total amount of all the other fire insurance agencies put together —outside Lloyd's—amounts to another £5,000,000; but we can have no certainty upon that head, because many of them publish no figures of any kind, some being in the nature of mutual aid societies and others sectarian.

The accumulated funds may not seem excessive in view of the fact that the value of the property of all descriptions insured against fire the world over runs into thousands of millions sterling, and that the British share of the business done is a preponderating one. The accumulations, however, have proved to be ample against all ordinary contingencies, and it was only when our offices went abroad, to the United States especially and to the colonies also, that the losses frequently threatened to sweep the funds in hand away and drove some companies to the wall or into amalgamation. Happily the days of this dangerous kind of expansion appear to be at an end. The megalo-

maniac passion that early seized our fire offices
has nearly run its course and borne its fruit.
Contraction of risks is now the order of the day,
so far as risks in other lands are concerned, and
magnificent totals in commitments are more likely
to be attained by means of amalgamation and
concentration of resources than by the acceptance
of promiscuous and ill-measured hazards the
world over for the sake of piling up a dazzling
premium income.

With regard to what may be described as
"miscellaneous" risks, we have offices in this
country that devote their attention either exclusively or principally to the sale of policies
guaranteeing employers against loss through the
malversation of their servants, or, in some cases,
even against losses arising through the mistakes
of these servants. Necessarily a business of this
kind is much on all fours with the accident form
of insurance which has of late years come into
vogue, that is to say, it must be extremely difficult
to make a reliable average of the risks run. For
one thing, the number of the dishonest among the
clerks of bankers, stockbrokers, merchants, houses
of business of all descriptions, is happily always
small. There are, however, seasons when what

might be called an epidemic of dishonesty crops up. Times of excitement arise on the Stock Exchange, when the fever of speculation gets into the blood of the community, and men of all classes and degrees are tempted to run risks which land them in losses they cannot meet. During periods like these guarantee offices are liable to suffer heavy losses, and, just as with fire insurance, such offices tend to frame their scale of premium charges on the basis of the high-water mark of their losses. Even so the risks are not great, and the premiums charged look at least moderate. Whether they are so or not, this form of insurance is compulsory upon a considerable section of the community, and rightly so, for it in many instances opens the way to responsible employment to thousands of young men who otherwise might not be able to work their way up in the service of their masters.

CHAPTER VIII

INSURANCE BUSINESS IN OTHER
COUNTRIES

MANY things of an interesting and profitable character might be recorded about
the origin and development of various forms of
insurance business in other countries, but details
of the kind would be beyond the scope of this
little book. A few facts, however, are worth bringing into prominence, were it for no other reason
than that they serve to emphasise the lead taken
and held by the great insurance offices of this
country in all branches of business. It is claimed
by a writer in the *Dictionnaire du Commerce*,
issued by Messrs. Yves Guyot and Arthur
Raffalovich, that Italy led the way in life business
as it did in marine; but if that be the case, it cannot be added that Italy takes any prominent part
or maintains any distinguished position in any
branch of insurance to-day. France, on the other

hand, which systematically took up fire and life insurance much later than we did, shows considerable progress, especially in fire business. In life it has not distinguished itself so much, for there are barely half a dozen offices doing that kind of business within the republic that could be classed alongside at least three times as many offices in this country. And at one time France had a much better relative position in marine business than it appears to hold to-day. So far as I know, however, no English marine company does any appreciable business in France. There are apparently thirty-four native marine companies in the republic, twenty of them with their head office in Paris, and they do a large business, not only for their own marine, but in competition with the marine companies of other countries ; but they are in no instance equal in power and importance to the greater of our English marine companies. Yet I do not think that any British office has much share in the business of France. It is otherwise with the life business, where foreign competition with native offices is keen, partly because native offices have had, in recent years, to come under regulations as to Government inspection and limits of risks—regulations which the foreign companies have not yet been compelled to submit to. There are no less than six English companies possessing branches in Paris, the most go-ahead amongst them being the Gresham and the first established the Patriotic. Powerful British offices, the Royal and the Northern, have also branches in Paris, and we may presume do the cream of the business falling to aliens. France has also been invaded by United States, Belgian, Swiss, Austrian, Spanish, Dutch, and even Russian insurance companies doing various kinds of business, principally, however, in competition with the native fire offices. The total of the assets possessed by French life companies up to the latest date for which I have figures appears to be under £80,000,000, but then until after the Revolution it may be said that life insurance was impossible upon any important scale in France, and the real growth of this kind of business has taken place within the last seventy years.

Our own colonies possess several important offices doing life business in all its varieties, together with fire and marine companies, details about which need not be given. It may be stated that several of them, Australian and Canadian, now compete for business in the United Kingdom.

The characteristic of these life offices is vigorous management, great push and energy, accompanied by a high ratio of expenses, and they are all confronted in these times by a decrease in the rate of interest obtained upon their invested funds. While the rate of interest was high their, to us, extravagant-looking rates of expenditure may not have mattered so much ; but they will now have to become thrifty, not to say parsimonious, in this respect, if they are not to pass through a period of stagnant business and diminished attractiveness for those who wish to insure.   One or two of the largest Australian offices, however, are splendidly equipped, and so rich that nothing short of a collapse in the colonial governments whose securities they largely hold can bring them into discredit.   They, however, invest their money, to an extent that I fear must be considered dangerous, in colonial real estate mortgages, many of which must involve considerable risks through depreciation.   Some of our own offices have entered into competition with the native Australasian offices for possession of these mortgages, and have had cause to rue their enterprise.   Looking at the position of these colonial offices from the point of view of one in this country desirous of taking out a life policy, I should say that not one of those whose names are growing familiar here offers sufficient guarantee of stability to warrant the investment. That, indeed, is the broad lesson inculcated by the position of life insurance business in every country outside our own. The risks they run and the style in which they do business render them unattractive to people in this country accustomed to greater economy in expenditure and more conservative management.

It is when we come to the United States that the story of insurance in other countries really becomes interesting and picturesque. Some wag has declared that when a man fails in the United States as a politician, a lawyer, or a preacher, there always remains to him the founding of an insurance company, and certainly that has been a conspicuous industry during the past sixty years, to go no further back, within the American Union. I find, for instance, that upwards of 400 insurance companies came into being and went out of existence in the United States up to the end of 1900. There are still, however, nearly 190 insurance companies of all kinds doing business in the State of New York—life, fire, and marine—but the great majority of them are quite modern,

especially the life companies.   There is, however,
one old benefit institution in the city of Philadelphia, called the Presbyterian Ministers' Fund,
which dates from 1759, and is still a modest and
well-managed little corporation, whose funds never
attain to any great magnitude, but the management of which is extremely circumspect and
judicious.   It works its business at the cost of
about 12½ per cent. of the premium income, and
follows the excellent habit of writing off from
revenue whatever premiums may be paid upon
any stock purchased over par for its funds.   Of
marine and fire companies there are also several
of respectable antiquity in the American Union.
Two Pennsylvania companies, for instance, date
from 1794, and between that date and 1820 fully
half a dozen companies were organised which still
exist doing fire and marine business.   Altogether
there are upwards of sixty of these companies in
existence, but very few of them are of any magnitude, and a considerable part of the ocean marine
insurance business of the United States is in the
hands of British offices.   Were it not, indeed, for
the coasting trade and the lake, river, and canal
navigation of the United States, there would be
little business for the native marine insurance

L

companies to transact ; but most of them combine fire and fire-marine with purely marine business, so that they contrive to collect considerable revenues in the course of a year out of the American public.

As for United States life companies, to return to these, I have not found one, except the already-mentioned Presbyterian Fund, that works its business on a scale of expenditure within miles, it may be said, of the limit set in an earlier chapter. The vicious habit of paying high commissions appears to have laid hold of life insurance all over the American Union, with the consequence that even the oldest offices of high repute appear to be unable to bring the ratio of their current expenditure to premium income down below 20 per cent. I have tested their figures at various dates and under various conditions, and have not yet found one of the large offices conducting its business for anything less than from 23 to 25 and 30 per cent. of the premium income. One of the oldest of these offices is the Etna Life, of New England. It is a powerful and highly respectable office, and yet, thanks to the fashionable rates of commission paid, not only for new business, but for collecting the premiums of old business, its expenses come to about 24 per cent. of the premium income; and when we pass outside mere life insurance of the ordinary types and touch upon accident business, the rate of expenditure runs up to 45 and 50 per cent. of the premium income, and sometimes even beyond these limits. Such rates of expenditure necessarily cause the business done to be of a highly speculative description, and the companies or mutual offices are all driven to manœuvre so as to be in a position to capture large sums of money on lapsed policies. That is the ugliest feature of all in the life insurance business as carried on in the United States, and were it not for the amounts every year laid hold of in this manner, as a rule without compensation to the unfortunate victims, I do not think any one of these offices could long continue in existence. Assuredly not one could be profitable to the holders of life policies who endured to the end.

As in France, so in the United States English companies have for many years been keen competitors, but, as a rule, only in fire and marine business, and the experience of our fire offices over there has been so unfortunate from first to last, that the tendency now is for them to retire from the field. They are either giving up their

American agencies altogether, or transferring
their business in that part of the world to local
companies organised under the laws of one or
other of the States of the Union. It is to be
hoped that this withdrawal will be persevered with
until there is no longer any English company
competing for such business in any part of the
American Union. Canadian offices can continue
to fight for it if they please, but the habits of
business are so different, the speculation so daring
and competition so keen, the risks so tremendous
and often immeasurable compared with what we
are familiar with, whether at home or on the
continent of Europe, or even in Australia, that
our insurance managers are incapable of effectively
and profitably holding their own with the native
offices that swarm up and disappear like midges.
The results of competition with such have been
disastrous, one may say throughout, and the
source of severe loss to several of our most important and wealthy fire offices. I do not see
how better circumstances or more favourable conditions of business can be looked for in the near
future, and therefore hold the opinion that it
would be well for our offices to abandon megalo-
mania of this kind, and confine themselves to the

underwriting of risks whose extent they can in some measure make sure of.

The United States is the home of fantastic schemes and out-of-the-way devices for attracting money from the public under the guise of insuring this, that, or the other. It was from the United States that Europe got its assessment or fraternity class of companies, already dealt with, and there also great enterprise has been shown in developing the accident, fatality, indemnity, and other out-of-the-way or brand-new branches of insurance business. It is worthy of notice, however, that the employers' liability and accident branches of insurance business appear to have been introduced into the States from this country, for I find in the records of the insurance department of the State of New York a conspicuous place occupied by our Employers' Liability Assurance Corporation, the Scottish General Accident Assurance Corporation, the London Guarantee and Accident Company, and the Ocean Accident and Guarantee Corporation. Plenty of United States competitors with these have sprung up, and such will doubtless multiply with great rapidity ; but as yet none of them are particularly strong, for the simple reason that they are of such recent establishment.

Indiana, for instance, has a company devoted to casualty insurance which commenced business in 1897, and the Philadelphia Casualty Company only started in 1900. Up to now, therefore, it may be supposed that British offices doing this kind of business have had a pretty open field, but I do not contemplate their future with any great degree of confidence, because they are certain to find competition growing against them with every year of their stay in the Union, and in all probability the end will be heavy commitments, severe losses, and retirement with some wisdom gained at a great cost.

The sum of all this is that every country should do its own insuring, insurance being one of those commodities, if the phrase may be used, that in my opinion do not very well bear either exportation or importation. Each country knows its own circumstances, can measure its own wealth and power of accumulation, and should therefore see to its own insurance. This is unquestionably true so far as life insurance goes, and also true as regards fire insurance. Marine insurance, however, is of a more cosmopolitan description, and perhaps ought not to be included in this sweeping judgment. Nevertheless, I incline to think that

British marine offices would sometimes fare rather badly if they took large lines in the lake shipping of the United States or in the coasting trade of the Atlantic and Pacific. It is so difficult to supervise distant commitments of this description. Trustworthy agents in each country or district may be found, and yet the contracts accepted by companies may go wrong. Of one thing, however, I am perfectly sure, whatever shippers and shipowners may do, whatever owners of factories, warehouses, shops, residences, and so on may do, the man who wishes to make a provision for his old age or those who come after him ought to make it in companies of native origin. And that is my last word.

APPENDIX I

A STUDY of the following table may help readers to form their own estimates about the qualities of the numerous insurance offices competing for their patronage. The figures have for the most part been extracted from the latest reports issued by the offices of companies as critically analysed in the *Investors' Review* on their appearance, but in one or two cases the reports do not appear to have reached it. Therefore, as in the instance of the Standard Life Office, the figures occasionally date back to 1901, but this in no way affects the conclusions which those who have mastered the simple principles laid down in the text of this book to guide them may easily draw for themselves.

COMPANY.				Accumulated Funds.		Ratio of Expenses to Premium Income.
				£		%
Alliance	...	...	...	6,774,000	...	10
Atlas	...	...	...	1,733,206	...	13
British Equitable		...	...	1,825,412	...	26
City of Glasgow		...	...	2,648,244	...	16
Clergy Mutual		...	...	4,147,020	...	7
Clerical, Medical, and General			...	4,005,892	...	13
Colonial Mutual		...	...	2,706,829	...	25
Commercial Union		...	...	2,592,271	...	13·44
Eagle	...	...	...	2,536,114	...	16·66
Economic	...	...	...	4,244,214	...	13·62
English and Scottish Law Life			...	2,134,512	...	17·18

Company.			Accumulated Funds.		Ratio of Expenses to Premium Income.
			£		%
Equitable	...	...	4,861,316	...	7·01
Friends' Provident	...	...	3,032,667	...	9
Gresham	...	...	8,279,970	...	18·5
Guardian	...	...	3,136,891	...	13·66
Hand-in-Hand	...	...	1,743,521	...	11·85
Law Life	...	...	5,074,818	...	12·82
Law Union and Crown		...	4,050,929	...	13·86
Liverpool and London and Globe			3,682,002	...	10
London Life ...	...	...	4,618,760	...	4·74
Metropolitan...	...	...	2,121,440	...	7·6
National Mutual	...	...	2,608,072	...	14·6
National Provident	...	...	5,878,924	...	10·7
Northern	...	...	4,109,816	...	10
Norwich Union Life	...	...	4,737,755	...	15·23
Provident	...	...	3,401,876	...	14·5
Prudential	...	...	47,155,201	...	{ *10 †38·34
Royal	...	...	7,765,745	...	12·6
Royal Exchange	...	...	2,377,441	...	14·24
Scottish Amicable	...	...	4,375,375	...	13·88
Scottish Life...	...	...	725,754	...	15·3
Scottish Provident	...	...	12,403,398	...	12·8
Scottish Union and National		...	4,153,473	...	13·58
Scottish Widows' Fund		...	16,330,562	...	11·5
Standard	...	...	10,126,311	...	19·42
Star	...	...	5,616,642	...	14·2
Sun Life	...	...	4,391,354	...	16·1
Union	...	...	2,965,097	...	13·25
Yorkshire	...	...	1,040,413	...	16·6
National Mutual of Australia		...	3,460,470	...	24·2
Australian Mutual Provident		...	19,245,287	...	13
Mutual Life of Australasia		...	1,638,939	...	26·75
Equitable of the U.S. ...		...	66,800,000	...	27
Mutual of New York ...		...	70,000,000	...	30·5
New York Life	...	...	64,600,000	...	26·5

* Ordinary. † Industrial.

APPENDIX II

LIGHT ON LIFE OFFICE PROFITS AND "LOADINGS"

AT the recent Annual Meeting of the Clerical, Medical, and General Life Assurance Society, the new Chairman of the Board, Mr. John Coles, delivered a speech so full of light upon the business of life insurance that I think some portions of it worthy of presentation here. Mr. Coles is himself an actuary of long experience and great acumen, but perhaps because his walk in life has led him into other kinds of business, he is singularly free from that tendency to mystery and what I may call mathematical necromancy which mars the public utterances of so many men eminent in the profession. He believes in letting the clients of his office know how the magic is produced, and therefore his account of the progress of the Clerical and Medical is both fascinating and full of instruction. Readers will see now what "loading" means and how it is worked, how profits accumulate and why they are needed, and gather some idea likewise of the amount of vigilance constantly demanded from insurance managers, if they are to keep abreast of new ideas, and to preserve the funds rolling up under their care from undue depletion. The Clerical and Medical has always been famous for the skill with which its investments have been made and changed; and the present head of the office, Mr. Whittall, in this and other respects fully maintains the reputation of his predecessors.

In reading the subjoined extracts some may be disposed to ask, Why all this piling up of money? Is not the accumulation of profit beyond risks and the liability of promised bonuses an abstraction of some of the gains belonging to present members of the Society for the benefit of the future? Not necessarily; for it must not be forgotten that as the business of a life office expands its risks likewise expand. Moreover, the profit made is continuously becoming divisible among existing policy-holders, who, at the close of each quinquennium, get the bigger bonuses the more profits accrue. And yet no carefully managed life office can afford at any time to distribute all the savings it has gathered together. The hidden dangers must be provided against, the unknown. Who, ten years ago, could have foreseen the terrible disasters which have smitten the investment markets of the world during the past four years? Without margins of large accumulated profits no life office could hope to maintain its position, to fulfil its engagements, through good times and bad. The great investment market is always changing its appearance, is restless as the ocean, and occasionally subjected to storms more or less violent, and against the dangers arising from these storms the prudently managed life office must incessantly guard. In insuring others it has also to insure itself, and that is why it must accumulate and accumulate until its resources lift it beyond the reach of the unforeseen, enabling it to stand serene as a lighthouse built upon a rock, no matter what financial tempests rage.

With this by way of preface, I now invite attention to the subjoined extracts from the admirable speech of Mr. Coles :—

"I attribute in a great measure the prosperity of this Society to its always being willing to make alterations from time to time to meet the varying conditions by which we are surrounded. It seems now almost ancient history to point to the time when we first began to pay claims in cash without any delay. I think we were almost pioneers in that, and I am very proud indeed of the fact that we were so, or that we were amongst the first. It has been one of the most acceptable concessions to the insuring public. Then, as we travelled on a little way, we next granted policies which are good the whole world over : they are good for people who wish to go to the Cape in war time, and they are good for people who wish to go to the West Coast of Africa, or anywhere else. If they once hold a policy in this office they may go over the whole world.

"Next, a thing of large importance, we granted great facilities for renewal of lapsed policies. Sometimes a man will allow a policy to lapse from inadvertence, or from some other reason, and it was extremely hard upon him to sacrifice all the previous payments, therefore we gave great facilities indeed for the renewal of our policies when they had lapsed. Coming down to more recent times, we have issued what we call prime cost policies, which have been very popular. We have granted redemption assurances, whereby, if a man buys a lease, he can come here and pay an equal annual amount and so get back his capital when the lease runs out. Only the other day we published a new prospectus for the officers of the Army and Navy; that prospectus gives rates which can never be altered while the policy is running, a principle which I believe to be extremely acceptable.

" These are some of our improvements, and they show that we have no desire to stand still. We have made these improvements primarily to stand well with the public, but also to stand well with our 14,000 policy-holders. That we have succeeded in some measure in gaining the favour of the public and of our own policy-holders may be assumed from the fact that a large number, larger than usual, came here to insure last year without the intervention of any agent whatever. This tendency we wish if possible to encourage, because it helps us very much in the development of our business. As to the changes we have made, I may say that I do not think it is the wish of the Board to stand still even now, and I hope we shall never forget that 'the old order changeth, yielding place to new,' and that we shall from time to time be willing to meet the varying requirements of the public, and so alter our mode of procedure as to still keep abreast of the times and secure our full share of new business.

"I now come to the Report which is before you. In the second paragraph you will see that we speak of the development of the business last year. The times were not all we could wish by any means; our agents and our staff must have discovered that. The public had to bear a very heavy imperial taxation, besides a very large local taxation, and we also had disquieting politics. This all somewhat affected life assurance. At the same time, gentlemen, you will find by the following paragraph, which bristles with figures, that we did the largest net sum assured that we have ever done in our history. You will find that there was over £710,000 in sums assured, and the premium income was over £23,000.

"To those who like percentages it may occur to some that £23,000 divided into £710,000 will show an entrance rate of 3·1 per cent. This may seem a high initial rate, but when you consider that a very large volume of business is now done by offices under what is called the endowment principle, it enhances the averages of our whole premiums. Whether in time this will be somewhat neutralised in our case by the smaller premiums we receive from thrift policies I am not able to say; but I do know that our thrift business is gaining ground rapidly. It means small premiums, but they will last a long time with us, I hope. You will find that last year the claims were a little under £200,000, and in the previous year they were rather below that, but it is well to bear in mind that in 1899 we paid £240,000, and in 1900 we paid £276,000.

"In Paragraph 6 of the Report, we show the largest genuine saving we have ever made, £175,000 in the

year. These savings have now mounted up to four
millions. The Society was established in 1824, but it
was not until 1855 that we arrived at our first million.
That must have been a long and weary time to those of
that generation. In the next twenty years we added on
another million, which brought us down to 1875. In the
next sixteen years we added on another million, which
would bring us to 1891, and in the last twelve years we
have added on yet another million, and we have therefore
now arrived at four millions; in fact, we have doubled
twice in fifty years.

" We have three great streams running into what I may
call our reservoir, where we are accumulating our profits.
It is an open secret that we want to find in that bonus
reservoir, as I may call it, at the end of five years something like £600,000. That means £120,000 a year.
Therefore there is much food for reflection for those who
have the management of the Society in hand.

"The first stream running into this reservoir is the
stream that flows from surplus interest. We are able to
assume by our calculations and our tables that if we
make only 2½ per cent. on all our money henceforward,
we shall have enough to pay all our claims as they arise.
What is the fact? We make not only 2½ per cent., we
make 3½ per cent., or about £3 12s. after the heavy
income tax is paid. If we take 1 per cent., which will
be quite within the margin, as the difference for profit—
1 per cent. on four millions is an easy item to reckon—it
is £40,000 a year. £40,000 a year, as you will readily
see, at the end of five years amounts to £200,000, and
also there is the compound interest to be taken into

account. Therefore you will observe that from that source there is a never-failing spring of profit which is constantly accumulating.

"The next in importance is the one that comes from the rate of mortality. I know at the present moment that our rate of mortality is running very low indeed, especially during the last two years. I am quite convinced that if we keep at anything like £200,000 a year for these five years—or, say, a million in the five years—we shall have a very considerable sum indeed to the good as a profit on that particular department. I cannot at present give you a money value of this, but I know it will be very considerable, and we look upon that, next to the rate of interest, as a steady stream running into our accumulations.

"The third is what we call the difference of the 'loading.' That is technical. I think there are one or two eminent actuaries present, shareholders with us, who will recognise loading as an old personal friend, in whose presence they have possibly much comfort. The loading here, taking the whole of our business, is about 18 per cent. I am proud to say that we spend at the present time only 13 per cent., and it is on this spending we have to look with very great care indeed. The difference between 13 and 18 per cent., you will see, is 5 per cent., and that is 5 per cent. difference to the good. Our premium income, as you know, is about £325,000, and that gives about £16,000 a year profit from that source. £16,000 a year accumulated for five years will not come quite to £100,000 with compound interest, but it will not be very far off.

" These are the three main streams which are running
into what at the end of the time I might almost call a
lake, but which is now a reservoir, for division at the end
of every five years.   There is yet another small stream,
which is apt to dry up in the summer, or at any rate
sometimes, and that is one that comes from the
surrenders.   We do not like these, but people come and
surrender sometimes, and of course there is a profit left.
There is also the profit which we have had for a series
of years from the sale of investments, and that has of
course been added from time to time to our profits.   But
it is the three main points which I specially wish you to
carry away in your memories.   We want to keep up the
rate of interest as far as we can consistently with security,
which, as I have said before, is of primary importance.
We want to keep down the rate of expense that we may
gain by the margin of loading, and we want to do our
very best to keep down the rate of mortality as compared
with the tables under which we are working.

" You may say, Is there any leakage in those reservoirs?
I do not think that there is.   We have no loss whatever
on mortgages ; we have not had to write down any loss,
even on fluctuating securities.   That is a point which I
think you will see is of considerable importance.   Our
neighbours, I am sorry to say—because we rejoice in the
prosperity of our neighbours—many of them have made
heavy losses, and have to write down considerably the
market value of the securities they hold as compared
with cost prices.   We fortunately in early days bought a
considerable amount of railway debenture stock, and
that has remained with us until now, and it has never

M

fallen to the price we originally paid for it when we made these large purchases in the sixties. That has helped to save the position very much ; but even in subsequent years we have been extremely fortunate in our investments, and we stand to-day in the favourable position of having securities probably worth at least £200,000 more than they cost us."

APPENDIX III

PERHAPS a word about annuities might be useful. To buy an annuity is not, strictly speaking, to effect an insurance on one's life, but the business is none the less a closely allied one, and many life offices carry on an annuity branch.

What is meant by "buying an annuity"? It usually means that the purchaser has sunk so much capital in securing an annual payment of a stipulated sum which is treated as income, and practically it implies the extinction of the capital invested, and that nothing is left for the heirs of an annuitant.

Take an example. Suppose a man, aged sixty, to be possessed of £1,000 which he does not wish or require as a duty to leave to anybody. He might invest the money at 3 per cent. or 4 per cent. interest, and get from it an income of £30 or £40 per annum; but in that case, assuming the security to be good, the £1,000 would be left intact at his death and pass away to another owner whether he liked or not.

To obviate this danger, and at the same time to procure a larger annual revenue for immediate spending, the owner of this £1,000 can go to an insurance office, or to the Post Office, or to the Commissioners of the National Debt, and pay all his £1,000 away in exchange for an income which will represent the return to him of both capital and interest. According to the terms offered by the office he selects, the annual income thus secured may vary from £86 to £95 per annum.

It would take a long and intricate story to tell how this is done, but one or two points may be made clear enough. First of all, a man of the age of sixty has not a long "average expectation of life"—about fourteen years. Divide the £1,000 by fifteen, to be on the safe side, and we get a sum of nearly £66 15s. which could be paid yearly for this period of time before the whole capital was exhausted. We are thus a good way on towards the £85 or £90 annuity which the £1,000 is to buy; and here interest comes in to help. It works the opposite way, though, from the interest accumulating on hoarded life premiums. In this case, year by year sees the sum mounting up through the double operation of interest and compound interest on former accumulations, and the receipt of further premiums. But in the case of an annuity the capital originally sunk is each year or each quarter becoming less. For the first three months, perhaps, the £1,000 is intact, and may earn 3 or 4 per cent. per annum—say, a matter of £8 to £10—as the case may be, but at the beginning of the second year it is less by between £60 and £70. As it diminishes its interest-earning power grows proportionately smaller until, if the annuitant lives long, the whole capital may have disappeared as well as all the interest earned upon it, leaving the institution which sold the annuity with a loss.   On long livers annuity-granting offices do make losses; but unless they have miscalculated the rate of interest they get on the funds remaining in their custody they should gain on the average, because some annuitants die well before the capital they invested has been all eaten up.

One might go on to discuss "loadings" for expenses, a small item in annuity business; the reasons for different offers by different annuity - vending offices, and other points; but the whole matter may be summed up in the advice here offered.   Get terms from at least half a dozen offices before deciding upon the one to buy an annuity from, and never select the offices offering the highest sums without inquiring into their stability, the amount of their accumulated annuity funds, and the rate of interest they earn upon the whole of their hoardings.   It by no means follows that the cheapest office is always the best, and where a large sum of money is involved, money to be parted with for good and all, it is prudent to spread it over several offices, buying no more than from one-third to one-fifth of the total annuity from each.

For small annuities the Post Office often offers better terms than any insurance office proper, why, I do not know.   But there is always this advantage with the Post Office or the National Debt Commissioners, that they have the resources of the nation behind them.   Should the business done by these departments involve a loss, and it generally does, the nation has to make it good.

The recent advance in the rates of interest obtainable on good securities favours the buyer of an annuity who goes to insurance companies for it, because it enables them to grant better terms. But for many years before this change took place they rather lost money by this branch of their business—hit in two ways: by the extension of the average term of life and by the fall in the rates of interest. Hence many offices either discouraged annuity business or refused it altogether, and all of them became disposed to quote terms that looked niggardly. These terms still prevail in many places, as the offices naturally want to make up for past losses, but competition will modify them in time. Remember only that it is better far to take $5\frac{1}{2}$ or 6 per cent. from a good office than 7 or 8 per cent. from a poor one.

APPENDIX IV

FIRE INSURANCE

THOSE who desire fuller information on this branch of insurance business cannot do better than turn to the article "Fire Insurance," by Mr. David Deuchar, in the third volume of Mr. Lisle's *Encyclopædia of Accounting*, published by Messrs. Wm. Green and Sons. It is full of information and illustrative examples relating to the age of offices, the forms of policies, rates of premiums, and so on. As being of interest to the general reader, it may be noted that Mr. Deuchar estimates the approximate annual premium income of fire offices in the United Kingdom at £22,000,000, in the United States at £25,000,000, in Germany at £12,000,000, and in France at only £5,000,000. No other country possesses a business in fire insurance large enough to furnish a premium income of as much as £5,000,000 a year, but Russia comes near it with £4,500,000 and Austria with £4,000,000.

INDEX

PLYMOUTH
WILLIAM BRENDON AND SON
PRINTERS

A CATALOGUE OF BOOKS
METHUEN AND COMPANY
PUBLISHERS : LONDON
36 ESSEX STREET
W.C.

CONTENTS

JULY 1903

A CATALOGUE OF

MESSRS. METHUEN'S
PUBLICATIONS

◆

PART I.—GENERAL LITERATURE

Jacob Abbot. THE BEECHNUT BOOK. Edited by E. V. LUCAS. Illustrated. *Demy 16mo. 2s. 6d.* [Little Blue Books.

W. F. Adeney, M.A. See Bennett and Adeney.

Æschylus. AGAMEMNON, CHOEPHOROE, EUMENIDES. Translated by LEWIS CAMPBELL, LL.D., late Professor of Greek at St. Andrews. *5s.*
[Classical Translations.

Æsop. FABLES. With 380 Woodcuts by THOMAS BEWICK. *Fcap. 8vo. 3s. 6d. net.* [Illustrated Pocket Library.

W. Harrison Ainsworth. WINDSOR CASTLE. With 22 Plates and 87 Woodcuts in the Text by GEORGE CRUIKSHANK. *Fcap. 8vo. 3s. 6d.* [Illustrated Pocket Library.

G. A. Aitken. See Swift.

William Alexander, D.D., Archbishop of Armagh. THOUGHTS AND COUNSELS OF MANY YEARS. Selected from the writings of Archbishop ALEXANDER. *Square Pott 8vo. 2s. 6d.*

Bishop Andrewes, THE DEVOTIONS OF By F. E. BRIGHTMAN, M.A., of Pusey House, Oxford. *Crown 8vo. 6s.*

Aristophanes. THE FROGS. Translated into English by E. W. HUNTINGFORD, M.A., Professor of Classics in Trinity College, Toronto. *Crown 8vo. 2s. 6d.*

Aristotle. THE NICOMACHEAN ETHICS. Edited, with an Introduction and Notes, by JOHN BURNET, M.A., Professor of Greek at St. Andrews. *Demy 8vo. 15s. net.*
'We have seldom, if ever, seen an edition of any classical author in which what is held in common with other commentators is so clearly put, and what is original is of such value and interest.'—*Pilot.*

R. Ashton. THE PEELES AT THE CAPITAL. Illustrated. *Demy 16mo. 2s. 6d.* [Little Blue Books.

J. B. Atkins. THE RELIEF OF LADYSMITH. With 16 Plans and Illustrations. *Third Edition. Crown 8vo. 6s.*

J. B. Atlay. See R. H. Barham.

Jane Austen. PRIDE AND PREJUDICE. Edited by E. V. LUCAS. *Two Volumes. Pott 8vo. Each volume, cloth, 1s. 6d. net.; leather, 2s. 6d. net.* [Little Library.

NORTHANGER ABBEY. Edited by E. V. LUCAS. *Pott 8vo. Cloth, 1s. 6d. net.; leather, 2s. 6d. net.* [Little Library.

Constance Bache. BROTHER MUSICIANS. Reminiscences of Edward and Walter Bache. With 16 Illustrations. *Crown 8vo. 6s. net.*

R. S. S. Baden-Powell, Major-General. THE DOWNFALL OF PREMPEH. A Diary of Life in Ashanti, 1895. With 21 Illustrations and a Map. *Third Edition. Large Crown 8vo. 6s.*

THE MATABELE CAMPAIGN, 1896. With nearly 100 Illustrations. *Fourth and Cheaper Edition. Large Crown 8vo. 6s.*

Graham Balfour. THE LIFE OF ROBERT LOUIS STEVENSON. *Second Edition. Two Volumes. Demy 8vo. 25s. net.*
'Mr. Balfour has done his work extremely well—done it, in fact, as Stevenson himself would have wished it done, with care and skill and affectionate appreciation.'—*Westminster Gazette.*

S. E. Bally. A FRENCH COMMERCIAL READER. With Vocabulary. *Second Edition. Crown 8vo. 2s.*
[Commercial Series.

FRENCH COMMERCIAL CORRESPONDENCE. With Vocabulary. *Third Edition. Crown 8vo. 2s.*
[Commercial Series.

A GERMAN COMMERCIAL READER. With Vocabulary. *Crown 8vo. 2s.*
[Commercial Series.

GERMAN COMMERCIAL CORRE-SPONDENCE. With Vocabulary. *Crown 8vo. 2s. 6d.* [Commercial Series.

Elizabeth L. Banks. THE AUTO-BIOGRAPHY OF A 'NEWSPAPER GIRL.' With Portrait of the Author and her Dog. *Crown 8vo. 6s.*
'A picture of a strenuous and busy life, perhaps the truest and most faithful representation of the ups and downs of a lady journalist's career ever given to the public. A very lively and interesting book.'—*Daily Telegraph.*
'A very amusing, cheery, good-natured account of a young lady's journalistic struggle in America and London.'—*Times.*

R. H. Barham. THE INGOLDSBY LEGENDS. Edited by J. B. Atlay. *Two Volumes. Pott 8vo. Each volume, cloth, 1s. 6d. net; leather, 2s. 6d. net.*
[Little Library.

S. Baring-Gould, Author of 'Mehalah,' etc. THE LIFE OF NAPOLEON BONA-PARTE. With over 450 Illustrations in the Text, and 12 Photogravure Plates. *Gilt top. Large quarto. 36s.*
'The main feature of this gorgeous volume is its great wealth of beautiful photogravures and finely-executed wood engravings, constituting a complete pictorial chronicle of Napoleon I.'s personal history.'—*Daily Telegraph.*

THE TRAGEDY OF THE CÆSARS. With numerous Illustrations [from Busts, Gems, Cameos, etc. *Fifth Edition. Royal 8vo. 15s.*
'A most splendid and fascinating book on a subject of undying interest. It is brilliantly written, and the illustrations are supplied on a scale of profuse magnificence.' —*Daily Chronicle.*

A BOOK OF FAIRY TALES. With numerous Illustrations and Initial Letters by ARTHUR J. GASKIN. *Second Edition. Crown 8vo. Buckram. 6s.*

OLD ENGLISH FAIRY TALES. With numerous Illustrations by F. D. BEDFORD. *Second Edition. Crown 8vo. Buckram. 6s.*
'A charming volume.'—*Guardian.*

THE CROCK OF GOLD. Fairy Stories. *Crown 8vo. 6s.*
'Twelve delightful fairy tales.'—*Punch.*

THE VICAR OF MORWENSTOW: A Biography. A new and Revised Edition. With Portrait. *Crown 8vo. 3s. 6d.*
A completely new edition of the well-known biography of R. S. Hawker.

DARTMOOR: A Descriptive and Historical Sketch. With Plans and numerous Illustrations. *Crown 8vo. 6s.*
'A most delightful guide, companion and instructor.'—*Scotsman.*

THE BOOK OF THE WEST. With numerous Illustrations. *Two Volumes.* Vol. I. Devon. *Second Edition.* Vol. II. Cornwall. *Second Edition. Crown 8vo. 6s. each.*
'Bracing as the air of Dartmoor, the legend weird as twilight over Dozmare Pool, they give us a very good idea of this enchanting and beautiful district.'—*Guardian.*

A BOOK OF BRITTANY. With numerous Illustrations. *Crown 8vo. 6s.*
Uniform in scope and size with Mr. Baring-Gould's well-known books on Devon, Cornwall, and Dartmoor.

BRITTANY. Illustrated by Miss J. WYLIE. *Pott 8vo. Cloth, 3s.; leather, 3s. 6d. net.*
[Little Guides.
'A dainty representative of "The Little Guides."'—*Times.*
'An excellent little guide-book.'—*Daily News.*

OLD COUNTRY LIFE. With 67 Illustrations. *Fifth Edition. Large Cr. 8vo. 6s.*

AN OLD ENGLISH HOME. With numerous Plans and Illustrations. *Cr. 8vo. 6s.*

YORKSHIRE ODDITIES AND STRANGE EVENTS. *Fifth Edition. Crown 8vo. 6s.*

STRANGE SURVIVALS AND SUPER-STITIONS. *Second Edition. Cr. 8vo. 6s.*

A GARLAND OF COUNTRY SONG: English Folk Songs with their Traditional Melodies. Collected and Arranged by S. BARING-GOULD and H. F. SHEPPARD. *Demy 4to. 6s.*

SONGS OF THE WEST: Traditional Ballads and Songs of the West of England, with their Melodies. Collected by S. BARING-GOULD, M.A., and H. F. SHEP-PARD, M.A. In 4 Parts. *Parts I., II., III., 3s. each. Part IV., 5s. In One Volume, French Morocco, 15s.*
'A rich collection of humour, pathos, grace, and poetic fancy.'—*Saturday Review.*

Aldred F. Barker, Author of 'Pattern Analysis,' etc. AN INTRODUCTION TO THE STUDY OF TEXTILE DESIGN. With numerous Diagrams and Illustrations. *Demy 8vo. 7s. 6d.*

W. E. Barnes, D.D. ISAIAH. *Two Volumes. Fcap. 8vo. 2s. net each.* Vol. I. With Map. [Churchman's Bible.

Mrs. P. A. Barnett. A LITTLE BOOK OF ENGLISH PROSE. *Pott 8vo. Cloth, 1s. 6d. net; leather, 2s. 6d. net.*
[Little Library.

R. R. N. Baron, M.A. FRENCH PROSE COMPOSITION. *Crown 8vo. 2s. 6d. Key, 3s. net.*

MESSRS. METHUEN'S CATALOGUE

H. M. Barron, M.A., Wadham College, Oxford. TEXTS FOR SERMONS. With a Preface by Canon SCOTT HOLLAND. *Crown 8vo. 3s. 6d.*

C. F. Bastable, M.A., Professor of Economics at Trinity College, Dublin. THE COMMERCE OF NATIONS. *Second Edition. Crown 8vo. 2s. 6d.*
[*Social Questions Series.*

Mrs. Stephen Batson. A BOOK OF THE COUNTRY AND THE GARDEN. Illustrated by F. CARRUTHERS GOULD and A. C. GOULD. *Demy 8vo. 10s. 6d.*

A CONCISE HANDBOOK OF GARDEN FLOWERS. *Fcap. 8vo. 3s. 6d.*
See also Edward FitzGerald.

A Hulme Beaman. PONS ASINORUM; OR, A GUIDE TO BRIDGE. *Second Edition. Fcap. 8vo. 2s.*

W. S. Beard. JUNIOR ARITHMETIC EXAMINATION PAPERS. *Fcap. 8vo. 1s.* With or without Answers.
[*Junior Examination Series.*

Peter Beckford. THOUGHTS ON HUNTING. Edited by J. OTHO PAGET, and Illustrated by G. H. JALLAND. *Demy 8vo. 10s. 6d.*

William Beckford. THE HISTORY OF THE CALIPH VATHEK. Edited by E. DENISON ROSS. *Pott 8vo. Cloth, 1s. 6d. net; leather, 2s 6d. net.* [*Little Library.*

F. D. Bedford. See E. V. Lucas.

H. C. Beeching, M.A., Canon of Westminster. LYRA SACRA: A Book of Sacred Verse. Selected and Edited by. *Pott 8vo. Cloth, 2s.; leather, 2s. 6d.* [*Library of Devotion.*
See also Tennyson and Milton.

Jacob Behmen. THE SUPERSENSUAL LIFE. Edited by BERNARD HOLLAND. *Fcap. 8vo. 3s. 6d.*

Hilaire Belloc. PARIS. With Maps and Illustrations. *Crown 8vo. 6s.*

H. H. L. Bellot, M.A. THE INNER AND MIDDLE TEMPLE. With numerous Illustrations. *Crown 8vo. 6s. net.*
'A vast store of entertaining material.'—*Liverpool Mercury.*
'A delightful and excellently illustrated book; a real encyclopædia of Temple history.'—*Pilot.*

W. H. Bennett, M.A. A PRIMER OF THE BIBLE. *Second Edition. Crown 8vo. 2s. 6d.*
'The work of an honest, fearless, and sound critic, and an excellent guide in a small compass to the books of the Bible.'—*Manchester Guardian.*

W. H. Bennett and W. F. Adeney. A BIBLICAL INTRODUCTION. *Crown 8vo. 7s. 6d.*
'It makes available to the ordinary reader the best scholarship of the day in the field

of Biblical introduction. We know of no book which comes into competition with it.'—*Manchester Guardian.*

A. C. Benson, M.A. THE LIFE OF LORD TENNYSON. With 12 Illustrations. *Fcap. 8vo. Cloth, 3s. 6d.; Leather, 4s. net.* [*Little Biographies.*

R. M. Benson. THE WAY OF HOLINESS: a Devotional Commentary on the 119th Psalm. *Crown 8vo. 5s.*

E. R. Bernard, M.A., Canon of Salisbury. THE ENGLISH SUNDAY. *Fcap. 8vo. 1s. 6d.*

M. Bidez. See Parmentier.

C. Bigg, D.D. See St. Augustine, À Kempis, and William Law.

C. R. D. Biggs, B.D. THE EPISTLE TO THE PHILIPPIANS. Edited by. *Fcap. 8vo. 1s. 6d. net.* [*Churchman's Bible.*
'Mr. Biggs' work is very thorough, and he has managed to compress a good deal of information into a limited space.'—*Guardian.*

T. Herbert Bindley, B.D. THE OECUMENICAL DOCUMENTS OF THE FAITH. With Introductions and Notes. *Crown 8vo. 6s.*
A historical account of the Creeds.

William Blake. ILLUSTRATIONS OF THE BOOK OF JOB. Invented and Engraved by. *Fcap. 8vo. 3s. 6d. net.*
These famous Illustrations—21 in number—are reproduced in photogravure. 100 copies are printed on large paper, with India proofs and a duplicate set of the plates. *15s. net.* [*Illustrated Pocket Library.*
See also Little Library.

B. Blaxland, M.A. THE SONG OF SONGS. Being Selections from ST. BERNARD. *Pott 8vo. Cloth, 2s.; leather, 2s. 6d. net.* [*Library of Devotion.*

J. Harvey Bloom, M.A. SHAKESPEARE'S GARDEN. With Illustrations. *Fcap. 8vo. 2s. 6d.; leather, 3s. 6d. net.*
BY COMMAND OF THE KING

J. E. C. Bodley, Author of 'France.' THE CORONATION OF EDWARD VII. *Demy 8vo. 21s. net.*

George Body, D.D. THE SOUL'S PILGRIMAGE: Devotional Readings from his published and unpublished writings. Selected and arranged by J. H. BURN, B.D., F.R.S.E. *Pott 8vo. 2s. 6d.*

Arnold J. Boger. THE STORY OF GENERAL BACON: A Short Account of a Peninsula and Waterloo Veteran. *Crown 8vo. 6s.*

Cardinal Bona. A GUIDE TO ETERNITY. Edited with an Introduction and Notes, by J. W. STANBRIDGE, B.D., late Fellow of St. John's College, Oxford. *Pott 8vo. Cloth, 2s.; leather, 2s. 6d. net.* [*Library of Devotion.*

F. C. Boon, B.A. A COMMERCIAL GEOGRAPHY OF FOREIGN NATIONS. *Crown 8vo. 2s.*
[Commercial Series.

George Borrow. LAVENGRO. Edited by F. HINDES GROOME. *Two Volumes. Pott 8vo. Each volume, cloth, 1s. 6d. net; leather, 2s. 6d. net.* [Little Library.
ROMANY RYE. With Notes and an Introduction by JOHN SAMPSON. *Pott 8vo. Cloth, 1s. 6d. net; leather, 2s. 6d. net.*
[Little Library.

J. Ritzema Bos. AGRICULTURAL ZOOLOGY. Translated by J. R. AINSWORTH DAVIS, M.A. With an Introduction by ELEANOR A. ORMEROD, F.E.S. With 155 Illustrations. *Cr. 8vo. 3s. 6d.*

C. G. Botting, B.A. JUNIOR LATIN EXAMINATION PAPERS. *Fcap. 8vo. 1s.*
[Junior Examination Series.
EASY GREEK EXERCISES. *Cr. 8vo. 2s.*

E. M. Bowden. THE EXAMPLE OF BUDDHA: Being Quotations from Buddhist Literature for each Day in the Year. *Third Edition. 16mo. 2s. 6d.*

E. Bowmaker. THE HOUSING OF THE WORKING CLASSES. *Crown 8vo. 2s. 6d.* [Social Questions Series.

F. G. Brabant, M.A. SUSSEX. Illustrated by E. H. NEW. *Pott 8vo. Cloth, 3s.; leather, 3s. 6d. net.* [Little Guides.
'A charming little book; as full of sound information as it is practical in conception.' —*Athenæum.*
THE ENGLISH LAKES. Illustrated by E. H. NEW. *Pott 8vo. Cloth, 4s.; leather, 4s. 6d. net.* [Little Guides.

Miss M. Brodrick and Miss Anderson Morton. A CONCISE HANDBOOK OF EGYPTIAN ARCHÆOLOGY. With many Illustrations. *Crown 8vo. 3s. 6d.*

E. W. Brooks. See F. J. Hamilton.

C. L. Brownell. THE HEART OF JAPAN. Illustrated. *Crown 8vo. 6s.*
'These living pages are full of portraits from the life.'—*Morning Post.*
'It is the work of one who has lived in Japan among the people.'—*Athenæum.*
'A more readable and interesting book about Japan has not been written.'
—*Scotsman.*

Robert Browning. SELECTIONS FROM THE EARLY POEMS OF. With Introduction and Notes by W. HALL GRIFFIN. *Pott 8vo. 1s. 6d. net; leather, 2s. 6d. net.* [Little Library.

O. Browning, M.A. A SHORT HISTORY OF MEDIÆVAL ITALY, A.D. 1250-1530. *In Two Volumes. Crown 8vo. 5s. each.*
VOL. I. 1250-1409.—Guelphs and Ghibellines.
VOL. II. 1409-1530.—The Age of the Condottieri.

J. Buchan. See Isaak Walton.

Miss Bulley. See Lady Dilke.

John Bunyan. THE PILGRIM'S PROGRESS. Edited, with an Introduction, by C. H. FIRTH, M.A. With 39 Illustrations by R. ANNING BELL. *Cr. 8vo. 6s.*
'The best "Pilgrim's Progress."'—*Educational Times.*
GRACE ABOUNDING. Edited by C. S. FREER, M.A. *Pott 8vo. Cloth, 2s.; leather, 2s. 6d. net.* [Library of Devotion.

G. J. Burch, M.A., F.R.S. A MANUAL OF ELECTRICAL SCIENCE. With numerous Illustrations. *Crown 8vo. 3s.* [University Extension Series.

Gelett Burgess. GOOPS AND HOW TO BE THEM. With numerous Illustrations. *Small 4to. 6s.*

A. E. Burn, B.D., Examining Chaplain to the Bishop of Lichfield. AN INTRODUCTION TO THE HISTORY OF THE CREEDS. *Demy 8vo. 10s. 6d.* [Handbooks of Theology.
'This book may be expected to hold its place as an authority on its subject.'—*Spectator.*
See also Bishop Wilson.

J. H. Burn, B.D., F.R.S.E. A MANUAL OF CONSOLATION FROM THE SAINTS AND FATHERS. *Pott 8vo. Cloth, 2s.; leather, 2s. 6d. net.*
[Library of Devotion.

Robert Burns, THE POEMS OF. Edited by ANDREW LANG and W. A. CRAIGIE. With Portrait. *Second Edition. Demy 8vo, gilt top. 6s.*

J. B. Bury, LL.D. See Gibbon.

Alfred Caldecott, D.D. THE PHILOSOPHY OF RELIGION IN ENGLAND AND AMERICA. *Demy 8vo. 10s. 6d.* [Handbooks of Theology.
'A lucid and informative account, which certainly deserves a place in every philosophical library.'—*Scotsman.*

D. S. Calderwood, Headmaster of the Normal School, Edinburgh. TEST CARDS IN EUCLID AND ALGEBRA. In three packets of 40, with Answers. *1s. each.* Or in three Books, price *2d., 2d., and 3d.*

E.F.H. Capey. THE LIFE OF ERASMUS. With 12 Illustrations. *Cloth, 3s. 6d. net; leather, 4s. net.* [Little Biographies.

Thomas Carlyle. THE FRENCH REVOLUTION. Edited by C. R. L. FLETCHER, Fellow of Magdalen College, Oxford. *Three Volumes. Crown 8vo. 6s. each.* [Standard Library.
THE LIFE AND LETTERS OF OLIVER CROMWELL. With an Introduction by C. H. FIRTH, M.A., and Notes and Appendices by Mrs. S. C. LOMAS. *Three Volumes. Crown 8vo. 6s. each.* [Standard Library.

R. M. and A. J. Carlyle, M.A. BISHOP LATIMER. With Portrait. *Crown 8vo.* 3s. 6d. [Leaders of Religion.

C. C. Channer and M. E. Roberts. LACE-MAKING IN THE MIDLANDS, PAST AND PRESENT. With 16 full-page Illustrations. *Crown 8vo.* 2s. 6d.
'An interesting book, illustrated by fascinating photographs.'—*Speaker.*

Lord Chesterfield, THE LETTERS OF, TO HIS SON. Edited, with an Introduction, by C STRACHEV, and Notes by A. CALTHROP. *Two Volumes. Crown 8vo.* 6s. each. [Standard Library.

F W. Christian. THE CAROLINE ISLANDS. With many Illustrations and Maps. *Demy 8vo.* 12s. 6d. net.

Cicero. DE ORATORE I. Translated by E. N. P. MOOR, M.A. *Crown 8vo.* 3s. 6d. [Classical Translations.
SELECT ORATIONS (Pro Milone, Pro Murena, Philippic II., In Catilinam). Translated by H. E. D. BLAKISTON, M.A., Fellow and Tutor of Trinity College, Oxford. *Crown 8vo.* 5s. [Classical Translations.
DE NATURA DEORUM. Translated by F. BROOKS, M.A., late Scholar of Balliol College, Oxford. *Crown 8vo.* 3s. 6d. [Classical Translations.
DE OFFICIIS. Translated by G. B. GARDINER, M.A. *Crown 8vo.* 2s. 6d. [Classical Translations.

F. A. Clarke, M.A. BISHOP KEN. With Portrait. *Crown 8vo.* 3s. 6d. [Leaders of Religion.

A. L. Cleather and B. Crump. THE RING OF THE NIBELUNG : An Interpretation, embodying Wagner's own explanations. *Crown 8vo.* 2s. 6d.

G. Clinch. KENT. Illustrated by F. D. BEDFORD. *Pott 8vo. Cloth,* 3s. ; *leather,* 3s. 6d. net. [Little Guides.

T. Cobb. THE CASTAWAYS OF MEADOWBANK. Illustrated. *Demy 16mo.* 2s. 6d. [Little Blue Books.
THE TREASURY OF PRINCEGATE PRIORY. Illustrated. *Demy 16mo.* 2s. 6d. [Little Blue Books.

E. H. Colbeck, M.D. DISEASES OF THE HEART. With numerous Illustrations. *Demy 8vo.* 12s.

W. G. Collingwood, M.A. THE LIFE OF JOHN RUSKIN. With Portraits. *Cheap Edition. Crown 8vo.* 6s.

J. C. Collins, M.A. See Tennyson.

W. E. Collins, M.A. THE BEGINNINGS OF ENGLISH CHRISTIANITY. With Map. *Crown 8vo.* 3s. 6d. [Churchman's Library.

A. M. Cook, M.A. See E. C. Marchant.

R. W. Cooke-Taylor. THE FACTORY SYSTEM. *Crown 8vo.* 2s. 6d. [Social Questions Series.

William Coombe. THE TOUR OF DR. SYNTAX IN SEARCH OF THE PICTURESQUE. With 30 Coloured Plates by T. ROWLANDSON. *Fcap. 8vo.* 3s. 6d. net. 100 copies on large Japanese paper, 21s. net. [Illustrated Pocket Library.
THE HISTORY OF JOHNNY QUAE GENUS : The Little Foundling of the late Dr. Syntax. With 24 Coloured Plates by ROWLANDSON. *Fcap. 8vo.* 3s. 6d. net. 100 copies on large Japanese paper. 21s. net. [Illustrated Pocket Library.

Marie Corelli. THE PASSING OF THE GREAT QUEEN : A Tribute to the Noble Life of Victoria Regina. *Small 4to.* 1s.
A CHRISTMAS GREETING. *Sm. 4to.* 1s.

Rosemary Cotes. DANTE'S GARDEN. With a Frontispiece. *Second Edition. Fcap. 8vo. cloth* 2s. 6d. ; *leather,* 3s. 6d. net.

Harold Cox, B.A. LAND NATIONALIZATION. *Crown 8vo.* 2s. 6d. [Social Questions Series.

W. J. Craig. See Shakespeare.

W. A. Craigie. A PRIMER OF BURNS. *Crown 8vo.* 2s. 6d.

Mrs. Craik. JOHN HALIFAX, GENTLEMAN. Edited by ANNIE MATHESON. *Two Volumes. Pott 8vo. Each Volume, Cloth,* 1s. 6d. net ; *leather,* 2s. 6d. net. [Little Library.

Richard Crashaw, THE ENGLISH POEMS OF. Edited by EDWARD HUTTON. *Pott 8vo. Cloth,* 1s. 6d. net ; *leather,* 2s. 6d. net. [Little Library.

F. G. Crawford. See Mary C. Danson.

Mrs. Cross (Ada Cambridge). THIRTY YEARS IN AUSTRALIA. *Demy 8vo.* 7s. 6d.

B. Crump. See A. L. Cleather.

C. G. Crump, M.A. See Thomas Ellwood.

F. H. E. Cunliffe, Fellow of All Souls' College, Oxford. THE HISTORY OF THE BOER WAR. With many Illustrations, Plans, and Portraits. *In 2 vols. Vol. I.,* 15s.

E. L. Cutts, D.D. AUGUSTINE OF CANTERBURY. With Portrait. *Crown 8vo.* 3s. 6d. [Leaders of Religion.

The Brothers Dalziel. A RECORD OF FIFTY YEARS' WORK. With 150 Illustrations. *Large 4to.* 21s. net.
The record of the work of the celebrated Engravers, containing a Gallery of beautiful Pictures by F. Walker, Sir J. Millais, Lord Leighton, and other great Artists. The book is a history of the finest black-and-white work of the nineteenth century.

G. W. Daniell, M.A. BISHOP WILBER-FORCE. With Portrait. *Crown 8vo.*
3s. 6d. [Leaders of Religion.

Mary C. Danson and F. G. Crawford.
FATHERS IN THE FAITH. *Small 8vo.*
1s. 6d.

Dante Alighieri. LA COMMEDIA DI DANTE. The Italian Text edited by PAGET TOYNBEE, Litt.D., M.A. *Demy 8vo.*
Gilt top. 8s. 6d. *Also, Crown 8vo.* 6s.
[Standard Library.

THE INFERNO OF DANTE. Translated by H. F. CARY. Edited by PAGET TOYNBEE, Litt.D., M.A. *Pott 8vo. Cloth,*
1s. 6d. net; leather 2s. 6d. net.
[Little Library.

THE PURGATORIO OF DANTE. Translated by H. F. CARY. Edited by PAGET TOYNBEE, Litt.D., M.A. *Pott 8vo.*
Cloth, 1s. 6d. net; leather, 2s. 6d. net.
[Little Library.

THE PARADISO OF DANTE. Translated by H. F. CARY. Edited by PAGET TOYNBEE, Litt.D., M.A. *Pott 8vo. Cloth,*
1s. 6d. net; leather, 2s. 6d. net.
[Little Library.

See also Paget Toynbee.

A. C. Deane. A LITTLE BOOK OF LIGHT VERSE. Edited by. *Pott 8vo.*
Cloth, 1s. 6d. net; leather, 2s. 6d. net.
[Little Library.

SELECTIONS FROM THE POEMS OF GEORGE CRABBE. *Pott 8vo. Cloth,*
1s. 6d. net; leather, 2s. 6d. net.
[Little Library.

Percy Dearmer. See N. Hawthorne.

Leon Delbos. THE METRIC SYSTEM.
Crown 8vo. 2s.
A theoretical and practical guide, for use in schools and by the general reader.

Demosthenes: THE OLYNTHIACS AND PHILIPPICS. Translated upon a new principle by OTHO HOLLAND. *Crown 8vo.* 2s. 6d.

Demosthenes. AGAINST CONON AND CALLICLES. Edited with Notes and Vocabulary, by F. DARWIN SWIFT, M.A.
Fcap. 8vo. 2s.

Charles Dickens.
THE ROCHESTER EDITION.
Crown 8vo. Each Volume 3s. 6d. With Introductions by GEORGE GISSING, Notes by F. G. KITTON, and Topographical Illustrations.

THE PICKWICK PAPERS. With Illustrations by E. H. NEW. *Two Volumes.*
NICHOLAS NICKLEBY. With Illustrations by R. J. WILLIAMS. *Two Volumes.*
BLEAK HOUSE. With Illustrations by BEATRICE ALCOCK. *Two Volumes.*
OLIVER TWIST. With Illustrations by E. H. NEW.

THE OLD CURIOSITY SHOP. With Illustrations by G. M. BRIMELOW. *Two Volumes.*

BARNABY RUDGE. With Illustrations by BEATRICE ALCOCK. *Two Volumes.*

DAVID COPPERFIELD. With Illustrations by E. H. NEW. *Two Volumes.*

G. L. Dickinson, M.A., Fellow of King's College, Cambridge. THE GREEK VIEW OF LIFE. *Second Edition. Crown 8vo.*
2s. 6d. [University Extension Series.

H. N. Dickson, F.R.S.E., F.R.Met. Soc. METEOROLOGY. The Elements of Weather and Climate. Illustrated. *Crown 8vo.* 2s. 6d. [University Extension Series.

Lady Dilke, Miss Bulley, and Miss Whitley. WOMEN'S WORK. *Crown 8vo.*
2s. 6d. [Social Questions Series.

P. H. Ditchfield, M.A., F.S.A. ENGLISH VILLAGES. Illustrated. *Crown 8vo. 6s.*
'A book which for its instructive and pictorial value should find a place in every village library.'—*Scotsman.*

THE STORY OF OUR ENGLISH TOWNS. With Introduction by AUGUSTUS JESSOP, D.D. *Second Edition. Crown 8vo. 6s.*

OLD ENGLISH CUSTOMS: Extant at the Present Time. An Account of Local Observances, Festival Customs, and Ancient Ceremonies yet Surviving in Great Britain.
Crown 8vo. 6s.

W. M. Dixon, M.A. A PRIMER OF TENNYSON. *Second Edition. Crown 8vo. 2s. 6d.*
'Much sound and well-expressed criticism. The bibliography is a boon.'—*Speaker.*

ENGLISH POETRY FROM BLAKE TO BROWNING. *Second Edition. Crown 8vo.* 2s. 6d. [University Extension Series.

E. Dowden, Litt.D. See Shakespeare.

J. Dowden, D.D., Lord Bishop of Edinburgh. THE WORKMANSHIP OF THE PRAYER BOOK: Its Literary and Liturgical Aspects. *Second Edition.*
Crown 8vo. 3s. 6d. [Churchman's Library.

S. R. Driver., D.D., Canon of Christ Church, Regius Professor of Hebrew in the University of Oxford. SERMONS ON SUBJECTS CONNECTED WITH THE OLD TESTAMENT. *Crown 8vo. 6s.*
'A welcome companion to the author's famous "Introduction."'—*Guardian.*

S. J. Duncan (Mrs. COTES), Author of 'A Voyage of Consolation.' ON THE OTHER SIDE OF THE LATCH.
Second Edition. Crown 8vo. 6s.

J. T. Dunn, D.Sc., **and V. A. Mundella.**
GENERAL ELEMENTARY SCIENCE. With 114 Illustrations. *Crown 8vo. 3s. 6d.*
[Science Primers.

The Earl of Durham. A REPORT ON CANADA. With an Introductory Note. *Demy 8vo. 7s. 6d. net.*
A reprint of the celebrated Report which Lord Durham made to the British Government on the state of British North America in 1839. It is probably the most important utterance on British colonial policy ever published.

W. A. Dutt. NORFOLK. Illustrated by B. C. BOULTER. *Pott 8vo. Cloth, 3s.; leather, 3s. 6d. net.* [Little Guides.
THE NORFOLK BROADS. With coloured and other Illustrations by FRANK SOUTHGATE. *Large Demy 8vo. 21s. net.*

Clement Edwards. RAILWAY NATIONALIZATION. *Crown 8vo. 2s. 6d.* [Social Questions Series

W. Douglas Edwards. COMMERCIAL LAW. *Crown 8vo. 2s.* [Commercial Series.

H. E. Egerton, M.A. A HISTORY OF BRITISH COLONIAL POLICY. *Demy 8vo. 12s. 6d.*
'It is a good book, distinguished by accuracy in detail, clear arrangement of facts, and a broad grasp of principles.'—*Manchester Guardian.*

C. G. Ellaby. ROME. Illustrated by B. C. BOULTER. *Pott 8vo. Cloth, 3s.; leather, 3s. 6d. net.* [Little Guides.

Thomas Ellwood, THE HISTORY OF THE LIFE OF. Edited by C. G. CRUMP, M.A. *Crown 8vo. 6s.*
[Standard Library.
This edition is the only one which contains the complete book as originally published. It has a long Introduction and many Footnotes.

E. Engel. A HISTORY OF ENGLISH LITERATURE: From its Beginning to Tennyson. Translated from the German. *Demy 8vo. 7s. 6d. net.*

W. H. Fairbrother, M.A. THE PHILO-SOPHY OF T. H. GREEN. *Second Edition. Crown 8vo. 3s. 6d.*

Dean Farrar. See À Kempis.

Susan Ferrier. MARRIAGE. Edited by Miss GOODRICH FREER and Lord IDDES-LEIGH. *Two Volumes. Pott 8vo. Each volume, cloth, 1s. 6d. net; leather, 2s. 6d. net.* [Little Library.
THE INHERITANCE. *Two Volumes. Pott 8vo. Each Volume, cloth, 1s. 6d. net.; leather, 2s. 6d. net.* [Little Library.

W. S. Finn, M.A. JUNIOR ALGEBRA EXAMINATION PAPERS. *Fcap. 8vo. 1s.* [Junior Examination Series.

C. H. Firth, M.A. CROMWELL'S ARMY: A History of the English Soldier during the Civil Wars, the Commonwealth, and the Protectorate. *Crown 8vo. 7s. 6d.*

An elaborate study and description of Cromwell's army by which the victory of the Parliament was secured. The 'New Model' is described in minute detail.

G. W. Fisher, M.A. ANNALS OF SHREWSBURY SCHOOL. With numerous Illustrations. *Demy 8vo. 10s. 6d.*

Edward FitzGerald. THE RUBAIYAT OF OMAR KHAYYAM. With a Commentary by Mrs. STEPHEN BATSON, and a Biography of Omar by E. D. ROSS. *Crown 8vo. 6s.*

EUPHRANOR: A Dialogue on Youth. *32mo. Leather, 2s. net.* [Miniature Library.

E. A. FitzGerald. THE HIGHEST ANDES. With 2 Maps, 51 Illustrations, 13 of which are in Photogravure, and a Panorama. *Royal 8vo. 30s. net.*

W. H. Flecker, M.A., D.C.L., Headmaster of the Dean Close School, Cheltenham. THE STUDENTS' PRAYER BOOK. Part I. MORNING AND EVENING PRAYER AND LITANY. Edited by. *Crown 8vo. 2s. 6d.*

C. R. L. Fletcher. See Thomas Carlyle.

W. Warde Fowler. M.A. See Gilbert White.

J. F. Fraser. ROUND THE WORLD ON A WHEEL. With 100 Illustrations. *Fourth Edition Crown 8vo. 6s.*
'A classic of cycling, graphic and witty.'—*Yorkshire Post.*

S. C. Freer. See John Bunyan.

W. French, M.A., Principal of the Storey Institute, Lancaster. PRACTICAL CHEMISTRY. Part I. With numerous Diagrams. *Crown 8vo. 1s. 6d.*
[Textbooks of Technology.
'An excellent and eminently practical little book.'—*Schoolmaster.*

Ed. von Freudenreich. DAIRY BACTERIOLOGY. A Short Manual for the Use of Students. Translated by J. R. AINSWORTH DAVIS, M.A. *Second Edition. Revised. Crown 8vo. 2s. 6d.*

H. W. Pulford, M.A. THE EPISTLE OF ST. JAMES. Edited by. *Fcap. 8vo. 1s. 6d. net.* [Churchman's Bible.

Mrs. Gaskell. CRANFORD. Edited by E. V. LUCAS. *Pott 8vo. Cloth, 1s. 6d. net; leather, 2s. 6d. net.* [Little Library.

H. B. George, M.A., Fellow of New College, Oxford. BATTLES OF ENGLISH HISTORY. With numerous Plans. *Third Edition. Crown 8vo. 6s.*
'Mr. George has undertaken a very useful task—that of making military affairs intelligible and instructive to non-military readers—and has executed it with a large measure of success.'—*Times.*

H. de B. Gibbins, Litt.D., M.A. INDUSTRY IN ENGLAND: HISTORICAL OUTLINES. With 5 Maps. *Third Edition. Demy 8vo. 10s. 6d.*

A COMPANION GERMAN GRAMMAR. *Crown 8vo. 1s. 6d.*

THE INDUSTRIAL HISTORY OF ENGLAND. *Eighth Edition.* Revised. With Maps and Plans. *Crown 8vo. 3s.* [University Extension Series.

THE ECONOMICS OF COMMERCE. *Crown 8vo. 1s. 6d.* [Commercial Series.

COMMERCIAL EXAMINATION PAPERS. *Crown 8vo. 1s. 6d.* [Commercial Series.

BRITISH COMMERCE AND COLONIES FROM ELIZABETH TO VICTORIA. *Third Edition. Crown 8vo. 2s.* [Commercial Series.

ENGLISH SOCIAL REFORMERS. *Second Edition. Crown 8vo. 2s. 6d.* [University Extension Series.

H. de B. Gibbins, Litt.D., M.A., and **R. A. Hadfield,** of the Hecla Works, Sheffield. A SHORTER WORKING DAY. *Crown 8vo. 2s. 6d.* [Social Questions Series.

Edward Gibbon. THE DECLINE AND FALL OF THE ROMAN EMPIRE. A New Edition, edited with Notes, Appendices, and Maps, by J. B. BURY, LL.D., Fellow of Trinity College, Dublin. *In Seven Volumes. Demy 8vo. Gilt top, 8s. 6d. each. Also, Crown 8vo. 6s. each.*
'At last there is an adequate modern edition of Gibbon. . . . The best edition the nineteenth century could produce.'—*Manchester Guardian.*
'A great piece of editing.'—*Academy.* [Standard Library.

MEMOIRS OF MY LIFE AND WRITINGS. Edited, with an Introduction and Notes, by G. BIRKBECK HILL, LL.D. *Crown 8vo. 6s.*
'An admirable edition of one of the most interesting personal records of a literary life. Its notes and its numerous appendices are a repertory of almost all that can be known about Gibbon.'—*Manchester Guardian.* [Standard Library.

E. C. S. Gibson, D.D., Vicar of Leeds. THE BOOK OF JOB. With Introduction and Notes. *Demy 8vo. 6s.* [Westminster Commentaries.
'Dr. Gibson's work is worthy of a high degree of appreciation. To the busy worker and the intelligent student the commentary will be a real boon; and it will, if we are not mistaken, be much in demand. The Introduction is almost a model of concise, straightforward, prefatory remarks on the subject treated.'—*Athenæum.*

THE XXXIX. ARTICLES OF THE CHURCH OF ENGLAND. With an Introduction. *Third and Cheaper Edition in One Volume. Demy 8vo. 12s. 6d.* [Handbooks of Theology.

'We welcome with the utmost satisfaction a new, cheaper, and more convenient edition of Dr. Gibson's book. It was greatly wanted. Dr. Gibson has given theological students just what they want, and we should like to think that it was in the hands of every candidate for orders.'—*Guardian.*

THE LIFE OF JOHN HOWARD. With 12 Illustrations. *Fcap 8vo. Cloth, 3s. 6d. ; leather, 4s. net.* [Little Biographies.
See also George Herbert.

George Gissing. See Dickens.

A. D. Godley, M.A., Fellow of Magdalen College, Oxford. LYRA FRIVOLA. *Third Edition. Fcap. 8vo. 2s. 6d.*

VERSES TO ORDER. *Cr. 8vo. 2s. 6d. net.*

SECOND STRINGS. *Fcap. 8vo. 2s. 6d.*
A new volume of humorous verse uniform with *Lyra Frivola.*
'Neat, brisk, ingenious.'—*Manchester Guardian.*
'The verse is facile, the wit is ready.' *Daily Mail.*
'Excellent and amusing.'—*St. James's Gazette.*

Miss Goodrich-Freer. See Susan Ferrier.

H. L. Goudge, M.A., Principal of Wells Theological College. THE FIRST EPISTLE TO THE CORINTHIANS. Edited, with Introduction and Notes, by. *Demy 8vo. 6s.* [Westminster Commentaries.

P. Anderson Graham. THE RURAL EXODUS. *Crown 8vo. 2s. 6d.* [Social Questions Series.

F. S. Granger, M.A., Litt.D. PSYCHOLOGY. *Second Edition. Crown 8vo. 2s. 6d.* [University Extension Series.

THE SOUL OF A CHRISTIAN. *Crown 8vo. 6s.*
A book dealing with the evolution of the religious life and experiences.

E. M'Queen Gray. GERMAN PASSAGES FOR UNSEEN TRANSLATION. *Crown 8vo. 2s. 6d.*

P. L. Gray, B.Sc., formerly Lecturer in Physics in Mason University College, Birmingham. THE PRINCIPLES OF MAGNETISM AND ELECTRICITY : an Elementary Text-Book. With 181 Diagrams. *Crown 8vo. 3s. 6d.*

G. Buckland Green, M.A., Assistant Master at Edinburgh Academy, late Fellow of St. John's College, Oxon. NOTES ON GREEK AND LATIN SYNTAX. *Crown 8vo. 3s. 6d.*
Notes and explanations on the chief difficulties of Greek and Latin Syntax, with numerous passages for exercise.

E. T. Green, M.A. THE CHURCH OF CHRIST. *Crown 8vo. 6s.* [Churchman's Library

R. A. Gregory. THE VAULT OF HEAVEN. A Popular Introduction to Astronomy. With numerous Illustrations. *Crown 8vo.* 2s. 6d.
[University Extension Series.

W. Hall Griffin, M.A. See Robert Browning.

C. H. Grinling. A HISTORY OF THE GREAT NORTHERN RAILWAY, 1845-95. With Illustrations. *Demy 8vo.* 10s. 6d.

F. Hindes Groome. See George Borrow.

M. L. Gwynn. A BIRTHDAY BOOK. *Royal 8vo.* 12s.
This is a birthday-book of exceptional dignity, and the extracts have been chosen with particular care.

Stephen Gwynn. See Thackeray.

John Hackett, B.D. A HISTORY OF THE ORTHODOX CHURCH OF CYPRUS. With Maps and Illustrations. *Demy 8vo.* 15s. net.

A. C. Haddon, Sc.D., F.R.S. HEAD-HUNTERS, BLACK, WHITE, AND BROWN. With many Illustrations and a Map. *Demy 8vo.* 15s.
A narrative of adventure and exploration in Northern Borneo. It contains much matter of the highest scientific interest.

R. A. Hadfield. See H. de B. Gibbins.

R. N. Hall and W. G. Neal. THE ANCIENT RUINS OF RHODESIA. With numerous Illustrations. *Demy 8vo.* 21s. net.

F. J. Hamilton, D.D., **and E. W. Brooks.** ZACHARIAH OF MITYLENE. Translated into English. *Demy 8vo.* 12s. 6d. net.
[Byzantine Texts.

J. L. Hammond. CHARLES JAMES FOX: A Biographical Study. *Demy 8vo.* 10s. 6d.

D. Hannay. A SHORT HISTORY OF THE ROYAL NAVY, FROM EARLY TIMES TO THE PRESENT DAY. Illustrated. *Two Volumes. Demy 8vo.* 7s. 6d. each. Vol. I. 1200-1688.
See also R. Southey.

James O. Hannay, M.A. THE SPIRIT AND ORIGIN OF CHRISTIAN MONASTICISM. *Crown 8vo.* 6s.

A. T. Hare, M.A. THE CONSTRUCTION OF LARGE INDUCTION COILS. With numerous Diagrams. *Demy 8vo.* 6s.

Clifford Harrison. READING AND READERS. *Fcap. 8vo.* 2s. 6d.
'An extremely sensible little book.'— *Manchester Guardian.*

H. C. Hart. See Shakespeare.

Nathaniel Hawthorne. THE SCARLET LETTER. Edited by PERCY DEARMER. *Pott 8vo. Cloth,* 1s. 6d. net; *leather,* 2s. 6d net.
[Little Library.

Sven Hedin, Gold Medallist of the Royal Geographical Society. THROUGH ASIA. With 300 Illustrations from Sketches and Photographs by the Author, and Maps. *Two Volumes. Royal 8vo.* 36s. net.

T. F. Henderson. A LITTLE BOOK OF SCOTTISH VERSE. *Pott 8vo. Cloth,* 1s. 6d. net; *leather,* 2s. 6d. net.
[Little Library.

THE LIFE OF ROBERT BURNS. With 12 Illustrations. *Fcap. 8vo. Cloth,* 3s. 6d.; *leather,* 4s. net.
[Little Biographies.
See also D. M. Moir.

W. E. Henley. ENGLISH LYRICS. *Crown 8vo. Gilt top.* 3s. 6d.

W. E. Henley and C. Whibley. A BOOK OF ENGLISH PROSE. *Crown 8vo. Buckram, gilt top.* 6s.

H. H. Henson, B.D., Fellow of All Souls', Oxford, Canon of Westminster. APOSTOLIC CHRISTIANITY: As Illustrated by the Epistles of St. Paul to the Corinthians. *Crown 8vo.* 6s.

LIGHT AND LEAVEN: HISTORICAL AND SOCIAL SERMONS. *Crown 8vo.* 6s.

DISCIPLINE AND LAW. *Fcap. 8vo.* 2s. 6d.

THE EDUCATION ACT—AND AFTER. An Appeal addressed with all possible respect to the Nonconformists, Fellow-Guardians with English Churchmen of the National Christianity. *Crown 8vo.* 1s.

George Herbert. THE TEMPLE. Edited, with an Introduction and Notes, by E. C. S. GIBSON, D.D., Vicar of Leeds. *Pott 8vo. Cloth,* 2s.; *leather,* 2s. 6d. net.
[Library of Devotion.

Herodotus: EASY SELECTIONS. With Vocabulary. By A. C. LIDDELL, M.A. *Fcap. 8vo.* 1s. 6d.

W. A. S. Hewins, B.A. ENGLISH TRADE AND FINANCE IN THE SEVENTEENTH CENTURY. *Crown 8vo.* 2s. 6d.
[University Extension Series.

T. Hilbert. THE AIR GUN: or, How the Mastermans and Dobson Major nearly lost their Holidays. Illustrated. *Demy 16mo.* 2s. 6d.
[Little Blue Books.

Clare Hill, Registered Teacher to the City and Guilds of London Institute. MILLINERY, THEORETICAL, AND PRACTICAL. With numerous Diagrams. *Crown 8vo.* 2s.
[Textbooks of Technology.

Henry Hill, B.A., Headmaster of the Boy's High School, Worcester, Cape Colony. A SOUTH AFRICAN ARITHMETIC. *Crown 8vo.* 3s. 6d.
This book has been specially written for use in South African schools.

G. Birkbeck Hill, LL.D. See Gibbon.

Howard C. Hillegas. WITH THE BOER FORCES. With 24 Illustrations. *Second Edition. Crown 8vo. 6s.*

Emily Hobhouse. THE BRUNT OF THE WAR. With Map and Illustrations. *Crown 8vo. 6s.*

L. T. Hobhouse, Fellow of C.C.C., Oxford. THE THEORY OF KNOWLEDGE. *Demy 8vo. 21s.*

J. A. Hobson, M.A. PROBLEMS OF POVERTY: An Inquiry into the Industrial Condition of the Poor. *Fourth Edition. Crown 8vo. 2s. 6d.*
[Social Questions Series and University Extension Series.
THE PROBLEM OF THE UNEMPLOYED. *Crown 8vo. 2s. 6d.*
[Social Questions Series.

T. Hodgkin, D.C.L. GEORGE FOX, THE QUAKER. With Portrait. *Crown 8vo. 3s. 6d.* [Leaders of Religion.

Chester Holcombe. THE REAL CHINESE QUESTION. *Crown 8vo. 6s.*
'It is an important addition to the materials before the public for forming an opinion on a most difficult and pressing problem.'—*Times.*

Sir T. H. Holdich, K.C.I.E. THE INDIAN BORDERLAND : being a Personal Record of Twenty Years. Illustrated. *Demy 8vo. 15s. net.*
'Interesting and inspiriting from cover to cover, it will assuredly take its place as the classical work on the history of the Indian frontier.'—*Pilot.*

W. S. Holdsworth, M.A. A HISTORY OF ENGLISH LAW. *In Two Volumes. Vol. I. Demy 8vo. 10s. 6d. net.*

Canon Scott Holland. LYRA APOSTOLICA. With an Introduction. Notes by H. C. BEECHING, M.A. *Pott 8vo. Cloth, 2s.; leather, 2s. 6d. net.*
[Library of Devotion.

G. J. Holyoake. THE CO-OPERATIVE MOVEMENT TO-DAY. *Third Edition. Crown 8vo. 2s. 6d.*
[Social Questions Series.

Horace: THE ODES AND EPODES. Translated by A. D. GODLEY, M.A., Fellow of Magdalen College, Oxford. *Crown 8vo. 2s.* [Classical Translations.

E. L. S. Horsburgh, M.A. WATERLOO : A Narrative and Criticism. With Plans. *Second Edition. Crown 8vo. 5s.*
'A brilliant essay—simple, sound, and thorough.'—*Daily Chronicle.*
THE LIFE OF SAVONAROLA. With Portraits and Illustrations. *Second Edition. Fcap. 8vo. Cloth, 3s. 6d.; leather, 4s. net.* [Little Biographies.

R. F. Horton, D.D. JOHN HOWE. With Portrait. *Crown 8vo. 3s. 6d.* [Leaders of Religion.

Alexander Hosie. MANCHURIA. With Illustrations and a Map. *Demy 8vo. 10s. 6d. net.*

G. Howell. TRADE UNIONISM—NEW AND OLD. *Third Edition. Crown 8vo. 2s. 6d.* [Social Questions Series.

John Hughes. THE EDUCATIONAL SYSTEM OF ENGLAND AND WALES. With a Prefatory Note by ELLIS J. GRIFFITH, M.P. *Crown 8vo. 3s. 6d.*

A. W. Hutton, M.A. CARDINAL MANNING. With Portrait. *Crown 8vo. 3s. 6d.* [Leaders of Religion.
See also TAULER.

Edward Hutton. See Richard Crashaw.

R. H. Hutton. CARDINAL NEWMAN. With Portrait. *Crown 8vo. 3s. 6d.* [Leaders of Religion.

W. H. Hutton, M.A. THE LIFE OF SIR THOMAS MORE. With Portraits. *Second Edition. Crown 8vo. 5s.*
WILLIAM LAUD. With Portrait. *Second Edition. Crown 8vo. 3s. 6d.* [Leaders of Religion.

F. A. Hyett. A SHORT HISTORY OF FLORENCE. *Demy 8vo. 7s. 6d.*

Henrik Ibsen. BRAND. A Drama. Translated by WILLIAM WILSON. *Third Edition. Crown 8vo. 3s. 6d.*

Lord Iddesleigh. See Susan Ferrier.

W. R. Inge, M.A., Fellow and Tutor of Hertford College, Oxford. CHRISTIAN MYSTICISM. The Bampton Lectures for 1899. *Demy 8vo. 12s. 6d. net.*
'It is fully worthy of the best traditions connected with the Bampton Lectureship.'—*Record.*

A. D. Innes, M.A. A HISTORY OF THE BRITISH IN INDIA. With Maps and Plans. *Crown 8vo. 7s. 6d.*
'Written in a vigorous and effective style . . . a thoughtful and impartial account.'—*Spectator.*

S. Jackson, M.A. A PRIMER OF BUSINESS. *Third Edition. Crown 8vo. 1s. 6d.* [Commercial Series.

F. Jacob, M.A. JUNIOR FRENCH EXAMINATION PAPERS. *Fcap. 8vo. 1s.* [Junior Examination Series.

J. Stephen Jeans. TRUSTS, POOLS, AND CORNERS. *Crown 8vo. 2s. 6d.* [Social Questions Series.

E. Jenks, M.A., Professor of Law at University College, Liverpool. ENGLISH LOCAL GOVERNMENT. *Crown 8vo. 2s. 6d.* [University Extension Series.

C. S. Jerram, M.A. See Pascal.

Augustus Jessopp, D.D. JOHN DONNE. With Portrait. *Crown 8vo.* 3s. 6d.
[Leaders of Religion.

F. B. Jevons, M.A., Litt.D., Principal of Hatfield Hall, Durham. EVOLUTION. *Crown 8vo.* 3s. 6d. [Churchman's Library.
AN INTRODUCTION TO THE HISTORY OF RELIGION. *Second Edition. Demy 8vo.* 10s. 6d.
[Handbooks of Theology.
'The merit of this book lies in the penetration, the singular acuteness and force of the author's judgment. He is at once critical and luminous, at once just and suggestive. A comprehensive and thorough book.'—*Birmingham Post.*

Sir H. H. Johnston, K.C.B. BRITISH CENTRAL AFRICA. With nearly 200 Illustrations and Six Maps. *Second Edition. Crown 4to.* 18s. net.

H. Jones. A GUIDE TO PROFESSIONS AND BUSINESS. *Crown 8vo.* 1s. 6d.
[Commercial Series.

Lady Julian of Norwich. REVELATIONS OF DIVINE LOVE. Edited by GRACE WARRACK. *Crown 8vo.* 3s. 6d.
A partially modernised version, from the MS. in the British Museum of a book which Mr. Inge in his Bampton Lectures calls 'The beautiful but little known *Revelations.*'

Juvenal, THE SATIRES OF. Translated by S. G. OWEN. *Crown 8vo.* 2s. 6d.
[Classical Translations.

M. Kaufmann. SOCIALISM AND MODERN THOUGHT. *Crown 8vo.* 2s. 6d. [Social Questions Series.

J. F. Keating, D.D. THE AGAPE AND THE EUCHARIST. *Crown 8vo.* 3s. 6d.

John Keble. THE CHRISTIAN YEAR. With an Introduction and Notes by W. LOCK, D.D., Warden of Keble College. Illustrated by R. ANNING BELL. *Second Edition. Fcap. 8vo.* 3s. 6d.; *padded morocco,* 5s.
THE CHRISTIAN YEAR. With Introduction and Notes by WALTER LOCK, D.D., Warden of Keble College. *Second Edition. Pott 8vo. Cloth,* 2s.; *leather,* 2s. 6d. net. [Library of Devotion.
LYRA INNOCENTIUM. Edited, with Introduction and Notes, by WALTER LOCK, D.D., Warden of Keble College, Oxford. *Pott 8vo. Cloth,* 2s.; *leather,* 2s. 6d. net.
[Library of Devotion.
'This sweet and fragrant book has never been published more attractively.'—*Academy.*

Thomas à Kempis. THE IMITATION OF CHRIST. With an Introduction by DEAN FARRAR. Illustrated by C. M. GERE. *Second Edition. Fcap. 8vo.* 3s. 6d.; *padded morocco,* 5s.

THE IMITATION OF CHRIST. A Revised Translation, with an Introduction by C. BIGG, D.D., late Student of Christ Church. *Third Edition. Pott 8vo. Cloth,* 2s.; *leather,* 2s. 6d. net.
[Library of Devotion.
A practically new translation of this book which the reader has, almost for the first time, exactly in the shape in which it left the hands of the author.
THE SAME EDITION IN LARGE TYPE. *Crown 8vo.* 3s. 6d.

James Houghton Kennedy, D.D., Assistant Lecturer in Divinity in the University of Dublin. ST. PAUL'S SECOND AND THIRD EPISTLES TO THE CORINTHIANS. With Introduction, Dissertations and Notes. *Crown 8vo.* 6s.

J. D. Kestell. THROUGH SHOT AND FLAME : Being the Adventures and Experiences of J. D. KESTELL, Chaplain to General Christian de Wet. *Crown 8vo.* 6s.

C. W. Kimmins, M.A. THE CHEMISTRY OF LIFE AND HEALTH. Illustrated. *Crown 8vo.* 2s. 6d.
[University Extension Series.

A. W. Kinglake. EOTHEN. With an Introduction and Notes. *Pott 8vo. Cloth,* 1s. 6d. net; *leather,* 2s. 6d. net.
[Little Library.

Rudyard Kipling. BARRACK-ROOM BALLADS. 73rd Thousand. *Crown 8vo.* 6s.; *leather,* 6s. net.
'Mr. Kipling's verse is strong, vivid, full of character. . . . Unmistakable genius rings in every line.'—*Times.*
'The ballads teem with imagination, they palpitate with emotion. We read them with laughter and tears : the metres throb in our pulses, the cunningly ordered words tingle with life ; and if this be not poetry, what is?'—*Pall Mall Gazette.*
THE SEVEN SEAS. 62nd Thousand. *Crown 8vo.* Buckram, gilt top, 6s.; *leather,* 6s. net.
'The Empire has found a singer ; it is no depreciation of the songs to say that statesmen may have, one way or other, to take account of them.'—
Manchester Guardian.

F. G. Kitton. See Dickens.

W. J. Knox Little. See St. Francis de Sales.

Charles Lamb, THE COMPLETE WORKS OF. Edited by E. V. LUCAS. With Numerous Illustrations. *In Seven Volumes. Demy 8vo.* 7s. 6d. each.
THE ESSAYS OF ELIA. With over 100 Illustrations by A. GARTH JONES, and an Introduction by E. V. LUCAS. *Demy 8vo.* 10s. 6d.
'This edition is in many respects of peculiar beauty.'—*Daily Chronicle.*

*ELIA, AND THE LAST ESSAYS OF
ELIA.* Edited by E. V. LUCAS. *Pott 8vo.
Cloth, 1s. 6d. net; leather, 2s. 6d. net.*
[Little Library.
THE KING AND QUEEN OF HEARTS:
An 1805 Book for Children. Illustrated by
WILLIAM MULREADY. A new edition, in
facsimile, edited by E. V. LUCAS. 1s. 6d.
This little book is a literary curiosity, and
has been discovered and identified as the
work of Charles Lamb by E. V. LUCAS.
It is an exact facsimile of the original
edition, which was illustrated by Mulready.

Professor Lambros. ECTHESIS
CHRONICA. Edited by. *Demy 8vo.
7s. 6d. net.* [Byzantine Texts.

Stanley Lane-Poole. THE LIFE OF
SIR HARRY PARKES. *A New and
Cheaper Edition. Crown 8vo. 6s.*
A HISTORY OF EGYPT IN THE
MIDDLE AGES. Fully Illustrated.
Crown 8vo. 6s.

F. Langbridge, M.A. BALLADS OF THE
BRAVE: Poems of Chivalry, Enterprise,
Courage, and Constancy. *Second Edition.
Crown 8vo. 2s. 6d.*
'The book is full of splendid things.'—
World.

William Law. A SERIOUS CALL TO A
DEVOUT AND HOLY LIFE. Edited,
with an Introduction, by C. BIGG, D.D.,
late Student of Christ Church. *Pott 8vo.
Cloth, 2s.; leather, 2s. 6d. net.*
[Library of Devotion.
This is a reprint, word for word and line
for line, of the *Editio Princeps.*

G. S. Layard. THE LIFE OF MRS.
LYNN LINTON. Illustrated. *Demy
8vo. 12s. 6d.*

Captain Melville Lee. A HISTORY OF
POLICE IN ENGLAND. *Crown 8vo.
7s. 6d.*
'A learned book, comprising many curious
details to interest the general reader as well
as the student who will consult it for exact
information.'—*Daily News.*

V. B. Lewes, M.A. AIR AND WATER.
Illustrated. *Crown 8vo. 2s. 6d.*
[University Extension Series.

W. M. Lindsay. See Plautus.

Walter Lock, D.D., Warden of Keble College. ST. PAUL, THE MASTER-
BUILDER. *Crown 8vo. 3s. 6d.*
See also Keble and Westminster Commentaries.
JOHN KEBLE. With Portrait. *Crown
8vo. 3s. 6d.* [Leaders of Religion.

George Horace Lorimer. LETTERS
FROM A SELF-MADE MERCHANT
TO HIS SON. *Crown 8vo. 6s.*

E. V. Lucas. THE VISIT TO LONDON.
Described in Verse, with Coloured Pic-
tures by F. D. BEDFORD. *Small 4to. 6s.*
This charming book describes the intro-
duction of a country child to the delights
and sights of London. It is the result of a
well-known partnership between author and
artist.
'A beautiful children's book.'
Black and White.
'The most inimitable verses and interest-
ing pictures.'—*Daily Chronicle.*
'Of quite unusual charm.'
Daily Telegraph.
See also Jane Austen and Mrs. Gaskell
and Charles Lamb.

Morton Luce. See Shakespeare.

Lucian. SIX DIALOGUES (Nigrinus,
Icaro-Menippus, The Cock, The Ship, The
Parasite, The Lover of Falsehood). Trans-
lated by S. T. Irwin, M.A., Assistant
Master at Clifton; late Scholar of Exeter
College, Oxford. *Crown 8vo. 3s. 6d.*
[Classical Translations.

L. W. Lyde, M.A. A COMMERCIAL
GEOGRAPHY OF THE BRITISH EM-
PIRE. *Third Edition. Crown 8vo. 2s.*
[Commercial Series.

Hon. Mrs. Lyttelton. WOMEN AND
THEIR WORK. *Crown 8vo. 2s. 6d.*
'Thoughtful, interesting, practical.'—
Guardian.
'The book is full of sound precept given
with sympathy and wit.'—*Pilot.*

Lord Macaulay. CRITICAL AND HIS-
TORICAL ESSAYS. Edited by F. C.
MONTAGUE, M.A. *Three Volumes. Cr.
8vo. 6s. each.* [Standard Library.
The only edition of this book completely
annotated.

J. E. B. M'Allen, M.A. THE PRINCIPLES
OF BOOKKEEPING BY DOUBLE
ENTRY. *Crown 8vo. 2s.*
[Commercial Series.

J. A. MacCulloch. COMPARATIVE
THEOLOGY. *Crown 8vo. 6s.*
[Churchman's Library.
'Most carefully executed, readable and
informing.'—*Scotsman.*

F. MacCunn. JOHN KNOX. With Portrait. *Crown 8vo. 3s. 6d.*
[Leaders of Religion.

A. S. M'Dowall. THE LIFE OF
CHATHAM. With 12 Illustrations. *Fcap.
8vo. Cloth, 3s. 6d.; leather, 4s. net.*
[Little Biographies.

A. M. Mackay. THE CHURCHMAN'S
INTRODUCTION TO THE OLD
TESTAMENT. *Crown 8vo. 3s. 6d.*
[Churchman's Library.
'The book throughout is frank and
courageous.'—*Glasgow Herald.*

M. Macmillan, M.A.   See Shakespeare.

Laurie Magnus, M.A.   A PRIMER OF WORDSWORTH. *Crown 8vo. 2s. 6d.*

J. P. Mahaffy, Litt.D.   A HISTORY OF THE EGYPT OF THE PTOLEMIES. Fully Illustrated. *Crown 8vo. 6s.*

F. W. Maitland, LL.D., Downing Professor of the Laws of England in the University of Cambridge.   CANON LAW IN ENGLAND. *Royal 8vo. 7s. 6d.*

H. E. Malden, M.A.   ENGLISH RECORDS. A Companion to the History of England. *Crown 8vo. 3s. 6d.*
THE ENGLISH CITIZEN: HIS RIGHTS AND DUTIES. *Crown 8vo. 1s. 6d.*

E. C. Marchant, M.A., Fellow of Peterhouse, Cambridge, and Assistant Master at St. Paul's School.   A GREEK ANTHOLOGY. *Second Edition. Crown 8vo. 3s. 6d.*

E. C. Marchant, M.A., and **A. M. Cook**, M.A.   PASSAGES FOR UNSEEN TRANSLATION. *Second Edition. Crown 8vo. 3s. 6d.*
   'We know no book of this class better fitted for use in the higher forms of schools.'—*Guardian.*

J. E. Marr, F.R.S., Fellow of St. John's College, Cambridge.   THE SCIENTIFIC STUDY OF SCENERY. *Second Edition. Illustrated. Crown 8vo. 6s.*
   'A volume, moderate in size and readable in style, which will be acceptable alike to the student of geology and geography and to the tourist.'—*Athenæum.*
AGRICULTURAL GEOLOGY. With numerous Illustrations. *Crown 8vo. 6s.*

A. J. Mason.   THOMAS CRANMER. With Portrait. *Crown 8vo. 3s. 6d.*
[Leaders of Religion.

George Massee.   THE EVOLUTION OF PLANT LIFE: Lower Forms. With Illustrations. *Crown 8vo. 2s. 6d.*
[University Extension Series.

C. F. G. Masterman, M.A.   TENNYSON AS A RELIGIOUS TEACHER. *Crown 8vo. 6s.*
   'A thoughtful and penetrating appreciation, full of interest and suggestion.'—*World.*

Annie Matheson.   See Mrs. Craik.

Emma S. Mellows.   A SHORT STORY OF ENGLISH LITERATURE. *Crown 8vo. 3s. 6d.*
   'A lucid and well-arranged account of the growth of English literature.'—*Pall Mall Gazette.*

L. C. Miall, F.R.S.   See Gilbert White.

E. B. Michell.   THE ART AND PRACTICE OF HAWKING. With 3 Photogravures by G. E. Lodge, and other Illustrations. *Demy 8vo. 10s. 6d.*

J. G. Millais.   THE LIFE AND LETTERS OF SIR JOHN EVERETT MILLAIS, President of the Royal Academy. With 319 Illustrations, of which 9 are Photogravure. *2 vols. Royal 8vo. 20s. net.*
   'This splendid work.'—*World.*
   'Of such absorbing interest is it, of such completeness in scope and beauty. Special tribute must be paid to the extraordinary completeness of the illustrations.'—*Graphic.*

C. T. Millis, M.I.M.E., Principal of the Borough Polytechnic College.   TECHNICAL ARITHMETIC AND GEOMETRY. With Diagrams. *Crown 8vo. 3s. 6d.* [Textbooks of Technology.

J. G. Milne, M.A.   A HISTORY OF ROMAN EGYPT. Fully Illustrated. *Crown 8vo. 6s.*

P. Chalmers Mitchell, M.A.   OUTLINES OF BIOLOGY. Illustrated. *Second Edition. Crown 8vo. 6s.*
   A text-book designed to cover the Schedule issued by the Royal College of Physicians and Surgeons.

D. M. Moir.   MANSIE WAUCH. Edited by T. F. Henderson. *Pott 8vo. Cloth, 1s. 6d. net; leather, 2s. 6d. net.*
[Little Library.

F. C. Montague, M.A.   See Macaulay.

H. E. Moore.   BACK TO THE LAND: An Inquiry into the cure for Rural Depopulation. *Crown 8vo. 2s. 6d.*
[Social Questions Series.

W. R. Morfill, Oriel College, Oxford.   A HISTORY OF RUSSIA FROM PETER THE GREAT TO ALEXANDER II. With Maps and Plans. *Crown 8vo. 7s. 6d.*
   This history, is founded on a study of original documents, and though necessarily brief, is the most comprehensive narrative in existence. Considerable attention has been paid to the social and literary development of the country, and the recent expansion of Russia in Asia.

R. J. Morich, late of Clifton College.   GERMAN EXAMINATION PAPERS IN MISCELLANEOUS GRAMMAR AND IDIOMS. *Sixth Edition. Crown 8vo. 2s. 6d.* [School Examination Series.
   A Key, issued to Tutors and Private Students only, to be had on application to the Publishers. *Second Edition. Crown 8vo. 6s. net.*

Miss Anderson Morton.   See Miss Brodrick.

H. C. G. Moule, D.D., Lord Bishop of Durham.   CHARLES SIMEON. With Portrait. *Crown 8vo. 3s. 6d.*
[Leaders of Religion.

M. M. Pattison Muir, M.A.   THE CHEMISTRY OF FIRE. The Elementary Principles of Chemistry. Illustrated. *Crown 8vo. 2s. 6d.*
[University Extension Series.

V. A. Mundella, M.A. See J. T. Dunn.

W. G. Neal. See R. N. Hall.

H. W. Nevinson. LADYSMITH: The Diary of a Siege. With 16 Illustrations and a Plan. *Second Edition. Crown 8vo. 6s.*

J. B. B. Nichols. A LITTLE BOOK OF ENGLISH SONNETS. *Pott 8vo. Cloth, 1s. 6d. net; leather, 2s. 6d. net.*
[Little Library.

Nimrod. THE LIFE AND DEATH OF JOHN MYTTON, ESQ. With 18 Coloured Plates by HENRY ALKEN and T. J. RAWLINS. *Fcap. 8vo. 3s. 6d. net.* 100 *copies on large Japanese paper,* 21s. net.
[Illustrated Pocket Library.

James Northcote, R.A., THE CONVERSATIONS OF, WITH JAMES WARD. Edited by ERNEST FLETCHER. With many Portraits. *Demy 8vo. 10s. 6d.*

A. H. Norway, Author of 'Highways and Byways in Devon and Cornwall.' NAPLES: PAST AND PRESENT. With 40 Illustrations by A. G. FERARD. *Crown 8vo. 6s.*

Mrs. Oliphant. THOMAS CHALMERS. With Portrait. *Crown 8vo. 3s. 6d.*
[Leaders of Religion.

C. W. Oman, M.A., Fellow of All Souls', Oxford. A HISTORY OF THE ART OF WAR. Vol. II.: The Middle Ages, from the Fourth to the Fourteenth Century. Illustrated. *Demy 8vo. 21s.*
'The whole art of war in its historic evolution has never been treated on such an ample and comprehensive scale, and we question if any recent contribution to the exact history of the world has possessed more enduring value.'—*Daily Chronicle.*

Prince Henri of Orleans. FROM TONKIN TO INDIA. Translated by HAMLEY BENT, M.A. With 100 Illustrations and a Map. *Crown 4to, gilt top. 25s.*

R. L. Ottley, M.A., late Fellow of Magdalen College, Oxon., and Principal of Pusey House. THE DOCTRINE OF THE INCARNATION. *Second and Cheaper Edition. Demy 8vo. 12s. 6d.*
[Handbooks of Theology.
'A clear and remarkably full account of the main currents of speculation. Scholarly precision . . . genuine tolerance . . . intense interest in his subject—are Mr. Ottley's merits.'—*Guardian.*

LANCELOT ANDREWES. With Portrait. *Crown 8vo. 3s. 6d.*
[Leaders of Religion.

J. H. Overton, M.A. JOHN WESLEY. With Portrait. *Crown 8vo. 3s. 6d.*
[Leaders of Religion.

M. N. Oxford, of Guy's Hospital. A HANDBOOK OF NURSING. *Crown 8vo. 3s. 6d.*
'The most useful work of the kind that we have seen. A most valuable and practical manual.'—*Manchester Guardian.*

W. C. C. Pakes. THE SCIENCE OF HYGIENE. With numerous Illustrations. *Demy 8vo. 15s.*
'A thoroughgoing working text-book of its subject, practical and well-stocked.'—*Scotsman.*

Prof. Léon Parmentier and M. Bidez. EVAGRIUS. Edited by. *Demy 8vo. 10s. 6d. net.* [Byzantine Texts.

Pascal, THE THOUGHTS OF. With Introduction and Notes by C. S. JERRAM. *Pott 8vo. 2s.; leather, 2s. 6d. net.*
[Library of Devotion.

George Paston. SIDELIGHTS ON THE GEORGIAN PERIOD. With many Illustrations. *Demy 8vo. 10s. 6d.*
'Touched with lightness and sympathy. We recommend this book to all who are tired with the trash of novels.'—*Spectator.*
'This book is the highly diverting product of research and compilation. It is a magazine of instructive and amusing information.'—*Academy.*

H. W. Paul. See Laurence Sterne.

E. H. Pearce, M.A. THE ANNALS OF CHRIST'S HOSPITAL. With many Illustrations. *Demy 8vo. 7s. 6d.*
'A well-written, copious, authentic history.'—*Times.*

R. E. Peary, Gold Medallist of the Royal Geographical Society. NORTHWARD OVER THE GREAT ICE. With over 800 Illustrations. 2 vols. Royal 8vo. 32s. net.
'His book will take its place among the permanent literature of Arctic exploration.' —*Times.*

Sidney Peel, late Fellow of Trinity College, Oxford, and Secretary to the Royal Commission on the Licensing Laws. PRACTICAL LICENSING REFORM. *Second Edition. Crown 8vo. 1s. 6d.*

G. H. Perris. THE PROTECTIONIST PERIL; or the Finance of the Empire. *Crown 8vo. 1s.*

M. Perugini. SELECTIONS FROM WILLIAM BLAKE. *Pott 8vo. Cloth, 1s. 6d. net; leather, 2s. 6d. net.*
[Little Library.

J. P. Peters, D.D. THE OLD TESTAMENT AND THE NEW SCHOLARSHIP. *Crown 8vo. 6s.*
[Churchman's Library.
'Every page reveals wide reading, used with soun. and scholarly judgment.'
—*Manchester Guardian.*

W. M. Flinders Petrie, D.C.L., LL.D., Professor of Egyptology at University College.
A HISTORY OF EGYPT, FROM THE EARLIEST TIMES TO THE PRESENT DAY. Fully Illustrated. *In six volumes. Crown 8vo. 6s. each.*
'A history written in the spirit of scientific precision so worthily represented by Dr. Petrie and his school cannot but promote sound and accurate study, and supply a vacant place in the English literature of Egyptology.'—*Times.*
VOL. I. PREHISTORIC TIMES TO XVITH DYNASTY. *Fifth Edition.*
VOL. II. THE XVIITH AND XVIIITH DYNASTIES. *Third Edition.*
VOL. IV. THE EGYPT OF THE PTOLEMIES. J. P. MAHAFFY, Litt.D.
VOL. V. ROMAN EGYPT. J. G. MILNE, M.A.
VOL. VI. EGYPT IN THE MIDDLE AGES. STANLEY LANE-POOLE, M.A.
RELIGION AND CONSCIENCE IN ANCIENT EGYPT. Fully Illustrated. *Crown 8vo. 2s. 6d.*
SYRIA AND EGYPT, FROM THE TELL EL AMARNA TABLETS. *Crown 8vo. 2s. 6d.*
EGYPTIAN TALES. Illustrated by TRISTRAM ELLIS. *In Two Volumes. Crown 8vo. 3s. 6d. each.*
EGYPTIAN DECORATIVE ART. With 120 Illustrations. *Crown 8vo. 3s. 6d.*
'In these lectures he displays rare skill in elucidating the development of decorative art in Egypt.'—*Times.*

Philip Pienaar. WITH STEYN AND DE WET. *Second Edition. Crown 8vo. 3s. 6d.*
A narrative of the adventures of a Boer telegraphist of the Orange Free State during the war.

Plautus. THE CAPTIVI. Edited, with an Introduction, Textual Notes, and a Commentary, by W. M. LINDSAY, Fellow of Jesus College, Oxford. *Demy 8vo. 10s. 6d. net.*
For this edition all the important MSS. have been re-collated. An appendix deals with the accentual element in early Latin verse. The Commentary is very full.

J. T. Plowden-Wardlaw, B.A., King's College, Cambridge. EXAMINATION PAPERS IN ENGLISH HISTORY. *Crown 8vo. 2s. 6d.*
[School Examination Series.
Frank Podmore. MODERN SPIRITUALISM. *Two Volumes. Demy 8vo. 21s. net.*
A History and a Criticism.
'A complete guide to a very complex subject.'—*Academy.*

'Of great scientific value and considerable popular interest.'—*Scotsman.*
'A masterpiece of scientific analysis and exposition. There is no doubt it will hold the field for a long time.'—*Star.*
'The entire book is characterised by the greatest candour and fairness, and affords pleasant reading upon an entrancing theme.'—*Public Opinion.*

A. W. Pollard. OLD PICTURE BOOKS. With many Illustrations. *Demy 8vo. 7s. 6d. net.*

M. C. Potter, M.A., F.L.S. A TEXTBOOK OF AGRICULTURAL BOTANY. Illustrated. *2nd Edition. Crown 8vo. 4s. 6d.* [University Extension Series.

An Old Potter Boy. WHEN I WAS A CHILD. *Crown 8vo. 6s.*

G. Pradeau. A KEY TO THE TIME ALLUSIONS IN THE DIVINE COMEDY. With a Dial. *Small quarto. 3s. 6d.*

G. Prance. See R. Wyon.

L. L. Price, M.A., Fellow of Oriel College, Oxon. A HISTORY OF ENGLISH POLITICAL ECONOMY. *Fourth Edition. Crown 8vo. 2s. 6d.* [University Extension Series.

"Q." THE GOLDEN POMP. A Procession of English Lyrics. Arranged by A. T. QUILLER COUCH. *Crown 8vo. Buckram. 6s.*

R. B. Rackham, M.A. THE ACTS OF THE APOSTLES. With Introduction and Notes. *Demy 8vo. 12s. 6d.*
[Westminster Commentaries.
'A really helpful book. Both introduction and commentary are marked by common sense and adequate knowledge.'—*Guardian.*

B. W. Randolph, D.D., Principal of the Theological College, Ely. THE PSALMS OF DAVID. With an Introduction and Notes. *Pott 8vo. Cloth, 2s.; leather, 2s. 6d. net.* [Library of Devotion.
A devotional and practical edition of the Prayer Book version of the Psalms.

Hastings Rashdall, M.A., Fellow and Tutor of New College, Oxford. DOCTRINE AND DEVELOPMENT. *Crown 8vo. 6s.*

W. Reason, M.A. UNIVERSITY AND SOCIAL SETTLEMENTS. *Crown 8vo. 2s. 6d.* [Social Questions Series.

Charles Richardson. THE ENGLISH TURF. With numerous Illustrations and Plans. *Demy 8vo. 15s.*

M. E. Roberts. See C. C. Channer.

A. Robertson, D.D., Bishop of Exeter. REGNUM DEI. The Bampton Lectures of 1901. *Demy 8vo.* 12s. 6d. *net.*
'A notable volume. Its chief value and interest is in its historic treatment of its great theme.'—*Daily News.*
'It is altogether a solid piece of work and a valuable contribution to the history of Christian thought.'—*Scotsman.*

Sir G. S. Robertson, K.C.S.I. CHITRAL : The Story of a Minor Siege. With numerous Illustrations, Map and Plans. *Second Edition. Demy 8vo.* 10s. 6d.
'A book which the Elizabethans would have thought wonderful. More thrilling, more piquant, and more human than any novel.'—*Newcastle Chronicle.*

J. W. Robertson-Scott. THE PEOPLE OF CHINA. With a Map. *Crown 8vo.* 3s. 6d.

A. W. Robinson, M.A. THE EPISTLE TO THE GALATIANS. Explained. *Fcap. 8vo.* 1s. 6d. *net.* [Churchman's Bible.
'The most attractive, sensible, and instructive manual for people at large, which we have ever seen.'—*Church Gazette.*

Cecilia Robinson. THE MINISTRY OF DEACONESSES. With an Introduction by the Archbishop of Canterbury. *Crown 8vo.* 3s. 6d.

G. Rodwell, B.A. NEW TESTAMENT GREEK. A Course for Beginners. With a Preface by WALTER LOCK, D.D., Warden of Keble College. *Fcap. 8vo.* 3s. 6d.

Fred Roe. ANCIENT COFFERS AND CUPBOARDS: Their History and Description. With many Illustrations. *Quarto.* £3, 3s. *net.*

E. S. Roscoe. ROBERT HARLEY, EARL OF OXFORD. Illustrated. *Demy 8vo.* 7s. 6d.
This is the only life of Harley in existence.

Edward Rose. THE ROSE READER. With numerous Illustrations. *Crown 8vo.* 2s. 6d. *Also in 4 Parts. Parts I. and II.* 6d. *each ; Part III.* 8d. *; Part IV.* 10d.
A reader on a new and original plan. The distinctive feature of this book is the entire avoidance of irregularly-spelt words until the pupil has thoroughly mastered the principle of reading, and learned its enjoyment. The reading of connected sentences begins from the first page, before the entire alphabet is introduced.

E. Denison Ross, M.A. See W. Beckford and Edward FitzGerald.

A. E. Rubie, M.A., Head Master of the Royal Naval School, Eltham. THE GOSPEL ACCORDING TO ST. MARK. Edited by. With three Maps. *Crown 8vo.* 1s. 6d. [Junior School Books.

THE ACTS OF THE APOSTLES. *Crown 8vo.* 2s. [Junior School Books.

W. Clark Russell. THE LIFE OF ADMIRAL LORD COLLINGWOOD. With Illustrations by F. BRANGWYN. *Fourth Edition. Crown 8vo.* 6s.
'A book which we should like to see in the hands of every boy in the country.'—*St. James's Gazette.*

St. Anselm, THE DEVOTIONS OF. Edited by C. C. J. WEBB, M.A. *Pott 8vo.* Cloth, 2s. ; leather, 2s. 6d. *net.*
[Library of Devotion.

St. Augustine, THE CONFESSIONS OF. Newly Translated, with an Introduction and Notes, by C. BIGG, D.D., late Student of Christ Church. *Third Edition. Pott 8vo.* Cloth, 2s ; leather, 2s. 6d. *net.*
[Library of Devotion.
'The translation is an excellent piece of English, and the introduction is a masterly exposition. We augur well of a series which begins so satisfactorily.'—*Times.*

Viscount St. Cyres. THE LIFE OF FRANÇOIS DE FENELON. Illustrated. *Demy 8vo.* 10s. 6d.
'We have in this admirable volume a most valuable addition to our historical portrait gallery.'—*Daily News.*

St. Francis de Sales. ON THE LOVE OF GOD. Edited by W. J. KNOX-LITTLE, M.A. *Pott 8vo.* Cloth, 2s. ; leather, 2s. 6d. *net.* [Library of Devotion.

A. L. Salmon. CORNWALL. Illustrated by B. C. BOULTER. *Pott 8vo.* Cloth, 3s. ; leather, 3s. 6d. *net.* [Little Guides.

J. Sargeaunt, M.A. ANNALS OF WESTMINSTER SCHOOL. With numerous Illustrations. *Demy 8vo.* 7s. 6d.

C. Sathas. THE HISTORY OF PSELLUS. *Demy 8vo.* 15s. *net.*
[Byzantine Texts.

H. G. Seeley, F.R.S. DRAGONS OF THE AIR. With many Illustrations. *Crown 8vo.* 6s.
A popular history of the most remarkable flying animals which ever lived. Their relations to mammals, birds, and reptiles, living and extinct, are shown by an original series of illustrations.

V. P. Sells, M.A. THE MECHANICS OF DAILY LIFE. Illustrated. *Crown 8vo.* 2s. 6d. [University Extension Series.

Edmund Selous. TOMMY SMITH'S ANIMALS. Illustrated by G. W. ORD. *Second Edition. Fcap. 8vo.* 2s. 6d.
'A quaint, fascinating little book : a nursery classic.'—*Athenæum.*

A 3

William Shakespeare.
THE ARDEN EDITION.
Demy 8vo. 3s. 6d. each volume. General
Editor, W. J. Craig. An Edition of
Shakespeare in single Plays. Edited with
a full Introduction, Textual Notes, and
a Commentary at the foot of the page.
  'No edition of Shakespeare is likely to
prove more attractive and satisfactory than
this one. It is beautifully printed and paged
and handsomely and simply bound.'—
                    St. James's Gazette.
HAMLET.   Edited by Edward Dowden,
  Litt.D
ROMEO AND JULIET.   Edited by
  Edward Dowden, Litt.D.
KING LEAR. Edited by W. J. Craig.
JULIUS CAESAR.   Edited by M. Mac-
  millan, M.A.
THE TEMPEST.   Edited by Morton
  Luce.
OTHELLO. Edited by H. C. Hart.
CYMBELINE. Edited by Edward Dowden.

A. Sharp. VICTORIAN POETS. *Crown
8vo. 2s. 6d.* [University Extension Series.

J. S. Shedlock. THE PIANOFORTE
SONATA: Its Origin and Development.
Crown 8vo. 5s.

Arthur Sherwell, M.A. LIFE IN WEST
LONDON. *Third Edition. Crown 8vo.
2s. 6d.* [Social Questions Series.

Evan Small, M.A. THE EARTH. An
Introduction to Physiography. Illustrated.
Crown 8vo. 2s. 6d.
            [University Extension Series.

Nowell C. Smith, M.A., Fellow of New
College, Oxford. SELECTIONS FROM
WORDSWORTH. *Pott 8vo. Cloth,
1s. 6d. net; leather, 2s. 6d. net.*
                    [Little Library.

F. J. Snell. A BOOK OF EXMOOR.
Illustrated. *Crown 8vo. 6s.*

Sophocles. ELECTRA AND AJAX.
Translated by E. D. A. Morshead, M.A.,
Assistant Master at Winchester. *2s. 6d.*
              [Classical Translations.

L. A. Sornet and M. J. Acatos, Modern
Language Masters at King Edward's School,
Birmingham. A JUNIOR FRENCH
GRAMMAR. [Junior School Books.

R. Southey. ENGLISH SEAMEN
(Howard, Clifford, Hawkins, Drake, Caven-
dish). Edited, with an Introduction, by
David Hannay. *Second Edition. Crown
8vo. 6s.*
  'A brave, inspiriting book.'—*Black and
White.*

C. H. Spence, M.A., Clifton College. HIS-
TORY AND GEOGRAPHY EXAM-
INATION PAPERS. *Second Edition.
Crown 8vo. 2s. 6d.*
            [School Examination Series.

W. A. Spooner, M.A., Warden of New College, Oxford. BISHOP BUTLER. With
Portrait. *Crown 8vo. 3s. 6d.*
            [Leaders of Religion.

J. W. Stanbridge, B.D., late Rector of Bain-
ton, Canon of York, and sometime Fellow of
St. John's College, Oxford. A BOOK OF
DEVOTIONS. *Pott 8vo. Cloth, 2s.;
leather, 2s. 6d. net.* [Library of Devotion.
  'It is probably the best book of its kind.
It deserves high commendation.'—*Church
Gazette.*
  See also Cardinal Bona.

'Stancliffe.' GOLF DO'S AND DONT'S.
Second Edition. Fcap. 8vo. 1s.

A. M. M. Stedman, M.A.
INITIA LATINA: Easy Lessons on Elementary Accidence. *Sixth Edition. Fcap.
8vo. 1s.*

FIRST LATIN LESSONS. *Seventh Edition. Crown 8vo. 2s.*

FIRST LATIN READER. With Notes
adapted to the Shorter Latin Primer and
Vocabulary. *Sixth Edition revised. 18mo.
1s. 6d.*

EASY SELECTIONS FROM CÆSAR.
The Helvetian War. *Second Edition.
18mo. 1s.*

EASY SELECTIONS FROM LIVY. Part I.
The Kings of Rome. *18mo. Second Edition. 1s. 6d.*

EASY LATIN PASSAGES FOR UNSEEN
TRANSLATION. *Eighth Edition.
Fcap. 8vo. 1s. 6d.*

EXEMPLA LATINA. First Exercises in
Latin Accidence. With Vocabulary. *Second
Edition. Crown 8vo. 1s.*

EASY LATIN EXERCISES ON THE
SYNTAX OF THE SHORTER AND
REVISED LATIN PRIMER. With
Vocabulary. *Ninth and Cheaper Edition,
re-written. Crown 8vo. 1s. 6d.* Key,
3s. net. Original Edition. 2s. 6d.

THE LATIN COMPOUND SENTENCE:
Rules and Exercises. *Second Edition.
Crown 8vo. 1s. 6d.* With Vocabulary. *2s.*

NOTANDA QUAEDAM: Miscellaneous
Latin Exercises on Common Rules and
Idioms. *Fourth Edition. Fcap. 8vo. 1s. 6d.*
With Vocabulary. *2s.* Key, *2s. net.*

LATIN VOCABULARIES FOR REPETI-
TION: Arranged according to Subjects.
Eleventh Edition. Fcap. 8vo. 1s. 6d.

A VOCABULARY OF LATIN IDIOMS.
18mo. Second Edition. 1s.

STEPS TO GREEK. *Second Edition, revised. 18mo. 1s.*

A SHORTER GREEK PRIMER. *Crown
8vo. 1s. 6d.*

EASY GREEK PASSAGES FOR UNSEEN TRANSLATION. *Third Edition, revised. Fcap. 8vo.* 1s. 6d.

GREEK VOCABULARIES FOR REPETITION. Arranged according to Subjects. *Third Edition. Fcap. 8vo.* 1s. 6d.

GREEK TESTAMENT SELECTIONS. For the use of Schools. With Introduction, Notes, and Vocabulary. *Third Edition. Fcap. 8vo.* 2s. 6d.

STEPS TO FRENCH. *Sixth Edition.* 18mo. 8d.

FIRST FRENCH LESSONS. *Sixth Edition, revised. Crown 8vo.* 1s.

EASY FRENCH PASSAGES FOR UNSEEN TRANSLATION. *Fifth Edition, revised. Fcap. 8vo.* 1s. 6d.

EASY FRENCH EXERCISES ON ELEMENTARY SYNTAX. With Vocabulary. *Second Edition. Crown 8vo.* 2s. 6d. KEY. 3s. *net.*

FRENCH VOCABULARIES FOR REPETITION : Arranged according to Subjects. *Tenth Edition. Fcap. 8vo.* 1s.

FRENCH EXAMINATION PAPERS IN MISCELLANEOUS GRAMMAR AND IDIOMS. *Twelfth Edition. Crown 8vo.* 2s. 6d. [School Examination Series. A KEY, issued to Tutors and Private Students only, to be had on application to the Publishers. *Fifth Edition. Crown 8vo.* 6s. *net.*

GENERAL KNOWLEDGE EXAMINATION PAPERS. *Fourth Edition. Crown 8vo.* 2s. 6d. [School Examination Series. KEY (*Second Edition*) issued as above. 7s. *net.*

GREEK EXAMINATION PAPERS IN MISCELLANEOUS GRAMMAR AND IDIOMS. *Sixth Edition. Crown 8vo.* 2s. 6d. [School Examination Series. KEY (*Third Edition*) issued as above. 6s. *net.*

LATIN EXAMINATION PAPERS IN MISCELLANEOUS GRAMMAR AND IDIOMS. *Eleventh Edition. Crown 8vo.* 2s. 6d. [School Examination Series. KEY (*Fourth Edition*) issued as above. 6s. *net.*

R. Elliott Steel, M.A., F.C.S. THE WORLD OF SCIENCE. Including Chemistry, Heat, Light, Sound, Magnetism, Electricity, Botany, Zoology, Physiology, Astronomy, and Geology. 147 Illustrations. *Second Edition. Crown 8vo.* 2s. 6d.

PHYSICS EXAMINATION PAPERS. *Crown 8vo.* 2s. 6d. [School Examination Series.

C. Stephenson, of the Technical College, Bradford, and **F. Suddards,** of the Yorkshire College, Leeds. ORNAMENTAL DESIGN FOR WOVEN FABRICS. Illustrated. *Demy 8vo. Second Edition.* 7s. 6d.

J. Stephenson, M.A. THE CHIEF TRUTHS OF THE CHRISTIAN FAITH. *Crown 8vo.* 3s. 6d. An attempt to present in clear and popular form the main truths of the Faith. The book is intended for lay workers in the Church, for educated parents and for teachers generally.

Laurence Sterne. A SENTIMENTAL JOURNEY. Edited by H. W. PAUL. *Pott 8vo. Cloth,* 1s. 6d. *net; leather,* 2s. 6d. *net.* [Little Library.

W. Sterry, M.A. ANNALS OF ETON COLLEGE. With numerous Illustrations. *Demy 8vo.* 7s. 6d.

Katherine Steuart. BY ALLAN WATER. *Second Edition. Crown 8vo.* 6s. 'A delightful mixture of fiction and fact, tradition and history. There is not a page which is not informing and not entertaining.' —*Spectator.* 'A charming book. —*Glasgow Herald.* 'Has a unique charm.'—*Pilot.* 'A unique series of historical pictures.'— *Manchester Guardian.*

R. L. Stevenson. THE LETTERS OF ROBERT LOUIS STEVENSON TO HIS FAMILY AND FRIENDS. Selected and Edited, with Notes and Introductions, by SIDNEY COLVIN. *Sixth and Cheaper Edition. Crown 8vo.* 12s. LIBRARY EDITION. *Demy 8vo.* 2 vols. 25s. *net.* 'Irresistible in their raciness, their variety, their animation . . . of extraordinary fascination. A delightful inheritance, the truest record of a "richly compounded spirit" that the literature of our time has preserved.'—*Times.*

VAILIMA LETTERS. With an Etched Portrait by WILLIAM STRANG. *Third Edition. Crown 8vo. Buckram.* 6s.

THE LIFE OF R. L. STEVENSON. See G. Balfour.

E. D. Stone, M.A., late Assistant Master at Eton. SELECTIONS FROM THE ODYSSEY. *Fcap. 8vo.* 1s. 6d.

Charles Strachey. See Chesterfield.

A. W. Streane, D.D. ECCLESIASTES. Explained. *Fcap. 8vo.* 1s. 6d. *net.* [Churchman's Bible. 'Scholarly, suggestive, and particularly interesting.'—*Bookman.*

Clement E. Stretton. A HISTORY OF THE MIDLAND RAILWAY. With numerous Illustrations. *Demy 8vo.* 12*s.* 6*d.*

H. Stroud, D.Sc., M.A., Professor of Physics in the Durham College of Science, Newcastle-on-Tyne. PRACTICAL PHYSICS. Fully Illustrated. *Crown 8vo.* 3*s.* 6*d.*
[Textbooks of Technology.

Capt. Donald Stuart. THE STRUGGLE FOR PERSIA. With a Map. *Crown 8vo.* 6*s.*

F. Suddards. See C. Stephenson.

Jonathan Swift. THE JOURNAL TO STELLA. Edited by G. A. AITKEN. *Crown 8vo.* 6*s.*   [Standard Library.

J. E. Symes, M.A. THE FRENCH REVOLUTION. *Crown 8vo.* 2*s.* 6*d.*
[University Extension Series.

Netta Syrett. A SCHOOL YEAR. Illustrated. *Demy 16mo.* 2*s.* 6*d.*
[Little Blue Books.

Tacitus. AGRICOLA. With Introduction, Notes, Map, etc. By R. F. DAVIS, M.A., late Assistant Master at Weymouth College. *Crown 8vo.* 2*s.*
GERMANIA. By the same Editor. *Crown 8vo.* 2*s.*
AGRICOLA AND GERMANIA. Translated by R. B. TOWNSHEND, late Scholar of Trinity College, Cambridge. *Crown 8vo.* 2*s.* 6*d.*   [Classical Translations.

J. Tauler. THE INNER WAY. Being Thirty-six Sermons for Festivals by JOHN TAULER. Edited, with an Introduction. By A. W. HUTTON, M.A. *Pott 8vo. Cloth,* 2*s.; leather,* 2*s.* 6*d. net.*
[Library of Devotion.

E. L. Taunton. A HISTORY OF THE JESUITS IN ENGLAND. With Illustrations. *Demy 8vo.* 21*s. net.*
'A history of permanent value, which covers ground never properly investigated before, and is replete with the results of original research. A most interesting and careful book.'—*Literature.*

F. G. Taylor, M.A. COMMERCIAL ARITHMETIC. *Third Edition. Crown 8vo,* 1*s.* 6*d.*   [Commercial Series.

Miss J. A. Taylor. THE LIFE OF SIR WALTER RALEIGH. With 12 Illustrations. *Fcap. 8vo. Cloth,* 3*s.* 6*d.; leather* 4*s. net.*   [Little Biographies.

T. M. Taylor, M.A., Fellow of Gonville and Caius College, Cambridge. A CONSTITUTIONAL AND POLITICAL HISTORY OF ROME. *Crown 8vo.* 7*s.* 6*d.*
'We fully recognise the value of this carefully written work, and admire especially the fairness and sobriety of his judgment and the human interest with which he has inspired his subject.'—*Athenæum.*

Alfred, Lord Tennyson. THE EARLY POEMS OF. Edited, with Notes and an Introduction, by J. CHURTON COLLINS, M.A. *Crown 8vo.* 6*s.*
[Standard Library.
Also with 10 Illustrations in Photogravure by W. E. F. BRITTEN. *Demy 8vo.* 10*s.* 6*d.*
An elaborate edition of the celebrated volume which was published in its final and definitive form in 1853.

IN MEMORIAM, MAUD, AND THE PRINCESS. Edited by J. CHURTON COLLINS, M.A. *Crown 8vo.* 6*s.*
[Standard Library.

MAUD. Edited by ELIZABETH WORDSWORTH. *Pott 8vo. Cloth,* 1*s.* 6*d. net; leather,* 2*s.* 6*d. net.*   [Little Library.

IN MEMORIAM. Edited, with an Introduction and Notes, by H. C. BEECHING, M.A. *Pott 8vo. Cloth,* 1*s.* 6*d. net; leather,* 2*s.* 6*d. net.*   [Little Library.

THE EARLY POEMS OF. Edited by J. C. COLLINS, M.A. *Pott 8vo. Cloth,* 1*s.* 6*d. net; leather,* 2*s.* 6*d. net.*   [Little Library.

THE PRINCESS. Edited by ELIZABETH WORDSWORTH. *Pott 8vo. Cloth,* 1*s.* 6*d. net; leather,* 2*s.* 6*d. net.*   [Little Library.

C. S. Terry. THE LIFE OF THE YOUNG PRETENDER. With 12 Illustrations. *Fcap. 8vo.* |*Cloth,* 3*s.* 6*d.; leather,* 4*s. net.*   [Little Biographies.

Alice Terton. LIGHTS AND SHADOWS IN A HOSPITAL. *Crown 8vo.* 3*s.* 6*d.*

W. M. Thackeray. VANITY FAIR. With an Introduction by S. GWYNN. *Three Volumes. Pott 8vo. Each volume, cloth,* 1*s.* 6*d. net; leather,* 2*s.* 6*d. net.*   [Little Library.

PENDENNIS. Edited by S. GWYNN. *Three Volumes. Pott 8vo. Each volume, cloth,* 1*s.* 6*d. net; leather,* 2*s.* 6*d. net.*   [Little Library.

ESMOND. Edited by STEPHEN GWYNN. *Two volumes. Pott 8vo. Each Volume, cloth,* 1*s.* 6*d. net; leather,* 2*s.* 6*d. net.*   [Little Library.

CHRISTMAS BOOKS. Edited by STEPHEN GWYNN. *Pott 8vo. Cloth,* 1*s.* 6*d. net; leather,* 2*s.* 6*d. net.*   [Little Library.

F. W. Theobald, M.A. INSECT LIFE. Illustrated. *Crown 8vo.* 2*s.* 6*d.*
[University Extension Series.

A. H. Thompson. CAMBRIDGE AND ITS COLLEGES. Illustrated by E. H. NEW. *Pott 8vo. Cloth,* 3*s.; leather,* 3*s.* 6*d. net.*   [Little Guides.
'It is brightly written and learned, and is just such a book as a cultured visitor needs.'—*Scotsman.*

H. W. Tompkins, F.R.H.S. HERTFORD-SHIRE. Illustrated by E. H. NEW. *Pott 8vo. Cloth, 3s.; leather, 3s. 6d. net.* [Little Guides.

Paget Toynbee, Litt.D., M.A. See Dante. DANTE STUDIES AND RESEARCHES. *Demy 8vo. 10s. 6d. net.*

THE LIFE OF DANTE ALIGHIERI. With 12 Illustrations. *Second Edition. Fcap. 8vo. Cloth, 3s. 6d.; leather, 4s. net.* [Little Biographies.

Herbert Trench. DEIRDRE WED: and Other Poems. *Crown 8vo. 5s.*

G. E. Troutbeck. WESTMINSTER ABBEY. Illustrated by F. D. BEDFORD. *Pott 8vo. Cloth, 3s.; leather, 3s. 6d. net.* [Little Guides.

'In comeliness, and perhaps in completeness, this work must take the first place.'—*Academy.*

'A really first-rate guide-book.'—*Literature.*

Gertrude Tuckwell. THE STATE AND ITS CHILDREN. *Crown 8vo. 2s. 6d.* [Social Questions Series.

Louisa Twining. WORKHOUSES AND PAUPERISM. *Crown 8vo. 2s. 6d.* [Social Questions Series.

E. A. Tyler, B.A., F.C.S. A JUNIOR CHEMISTRY. *Crown 8vo. 2s. 6d.* [Junior School Books.

G. W. Wade, D.D. OLD TESTAMENT HISTORY. With Maps. *Second Edition. Crown 8vo. 6s.*

'Careful, scholarly, embodying the best results of modern criticism, and written with great lucidity.'—*Examiner.*

Izaak Walton. THE LIVES OF DONNE, WOTTON, HOOKER, HERBERT AND SANDERSON. With an Introduction by VERNON BLACKBURN, and a Portrait. *3s. 6d.*

THE COMPLEAT ANGLER. Edited by J. BUCHAN. *Pott 8vo. Cloth, 1s. 6d. net; leather, 2s. 6d. net.* [Little Library.

D. S. Van Warmelo. ON COMMANDO. With Portrait. *Crown 8vo. 3s. 6d.*

'A fighting Boer's simple, straightforward story of his life on commando. . . . Full of entertaining incidents.'—*Pall Mall Gazette.*

Grace Warrack. See Lady Julian of Norwich.

Mrs. Alfred Waterhouse. A LITTLE BOOK OF LIFE AND DEATH. Edited by. *Second Edition. Pott 8vo. Cloth, 1s. 6d. net; leather, 2s. 6d. net.* [Little Library.

C. C. J. Webb, M.A. See St. Anselm.

F. C. Webber. CARPENTRY AND JOINERY. With many Illustrations. *Third Edition. Crown 8vo. 3s. 6d.*

'An admirable elementary text-book on the subject.'—*Builder.*

Sidney H. Wells. PRACTICAL MECHANICS. With 75 Illustrations and Diagrams. *Second Edition. Crown 8vo. 3s. 6d.* [Textbooks of Technology.

J. Wells, M.A., Fellow and Tutor of Wadham College. OXFORD AND OXFORD LIFE. By Members of the University. *Third Edition Crown 8vo. 3s. 6d.*

A SHORT HISTORY OF ROME. *Fourth Edition.* With 3 Maps. *Cr. 8vo. 3s. 6d.*

This book is intended for the Middle and Upper Forms of Public Schools and for Pass Students at the Universities. It contains copious Tables, etc.

'An original work written on an original plan, and with uncommon freshness and vigour.'—*Speaker.*

OXFORD AND ITS COLLEGES. Illustrated by E. H. New. *Fifth Edition. Pott 8vo. Cloth, 3s.; leather, 3s. 6d. net.* [Little Guides.

'An admirable and accurate little treatise, attractively illustrated.'—*World.*

Helen C. Wetmore. THE LAST OF THE GREAT SCOUTS ('Buffalo Bill'). With Illustrations. *Second Edition. Demy 8vo. 6s.*

'A narrative of one of the most attractive figures in the public eye.'—*Daily Chronicle.*

C. Whibley. See Henley and Whibley.

L. Whibley, M.A., Fellow of Pembroke College, Cambridge. GREEK OLIGARCHIES: THEIR ORGANISATION AND CHARACTER. *Crown 8vo. 6s.*

G. H. Whitaker, M.A. THE EPISTLE OF ST. PAUL THE APOSTLE TO THE EPHESIANS. Edited by. *Fcap. 8vo. 1s. 6d. net.* [Churchman's Bible.

Gilbert White. THE NATURAL HISTORY OF SELBORNE. Edited by L. C. MIALL, F.R.S., assisted by W. WARDE FOWLER, M.A. *Crown 8vo. 6s.* [Standard Library.

E. E. Whitfield. PRECIS WRITING AND OFFICE CORRESPONDENCE. *Second Edition. Crown 8vo. 2s.* [Commercial Series.

COMMERCIAL EDUCATION IN THEORY AND PRACTICE. *Crown 8vo. 5s.* [Commercial Series.

An introduction to Methuen's Commercial Series treating the question of Commercial Education fully from both the point of view of the teacher and of the parent.

Miss Whitley. See Lady Dilke.

W. H. Wilkins, B.A. THE ALIEN INVASION. *Crown 8vo. 2s. 6d.* [Social Questions Series.

W. Williamson. THE BRITISH GARDENER. Illustrated. *Demy 8vo. 10s. 6d.*

W. Williamson, B.A. JUNIOR ENGLISH EXAMINATION PAPERS. *Fcap. 8vo. 1s.* [Junior Examination Series.

A JUNIOR ENGLISH GRAMMAR. With numerous passages for parsing and analysis, and a chapter on Essay Writing. *Crown 8vo.* 2s. [Junior School Books.
A CLASS-BOOK OF DICTATION PASSAGES. *Seventh Edition. Crown 8vo.* 1s. 6d. [Junior School Books.
EASY DICTATION AND SPELLING. *Second Edition. Fcap. 8vo.* 1s.

E. M. Wilmot-Buxton. THE MAKERS OF EUROPE. *Crown 8vo.* 3s. 6d.
A Text-book of European History for Middle Forms.
'A book which will be found extremely useful.'—*Secondary Education.*

Bishop Wilson. SACRA PRIVATA. Edited by A. E. BURN, B.D. *Pott 8vo. Cloth,* 2s.; *leather,* 2s. 6d. *net.* [Library of Devotion.

Beckles Willson. LORD STRATHCONA: the Story of his Life. Illustrated. *Demy 8vo.* 7s. 6d.
'An admirable biography, telling in the happiest manner the wonderful career of this giant of empire.'—*Black and White.*
'We should be glad to see this work taken as a model for imitation. He has given us an excellent and quite adequate account of the life of the distinguished Scotsman.'—*World.*

Richard Wilton, M.A., Canon of York. LYRA PASTORALIS: Songs of Nature, Church, and Home. *Pott 8vo.* 2s. 6d.
A volume of devotional poems.

S. E. Winbolt, M.A., Assistant Master in Christ's Hospital. EXERCISES IN LATIN ACCIDENCE. *Crown 8vo.* 1s.6d.
An elementary book adapted for Lower Forms to accompany the Shorter Latin Primer.

B. C. A. Windle, F.R.S., D.Sc. SHAKE-SPEARE'S COUNTRY. Illustrated by E. H. NEW. *Second Edition. Pott 8vo. Cloth,* 3s.; *leather,* 3s. 6d. *net.* [Little Guides.
'One of the most charming guide books. Both for the library and as a travelling companion the book is equally choice and serviceable.'—*Academy.*

THE MALVERN COUNTRY. Illustrated by E. H. NEW. *Pott 8vo. Cloth,* 3s.; *leather,* 3s. 6d. *net.* [Little Guides.

Canon Winterbotham, M.A., B.Sc., LL.B. THE KINGDOM OF HEAVEN HERE AND HEREAFTER. *Crown 8vo.* 3s. 6d. [Churchman's Library.

J. A. E. Wood. HOW TO MAKE A DRESS. Illustrated. *Second Edition. Crown 8vo.* 1s. 6d. [Textbooks of Technology.

Elizabeth Wordsworth. See Tennyson.

Arthur Wright, M.A., Fellow of Queen's College, Cambridge. SOME NEW TESTAMENT PROBLEMS. *Crown 8vo.* 6s. [Churchman's Library.

Sophie Wright. GERMAN VOCABU-LARIES FOR REPETITION. *Fcap. 8vo.* 1s. 6d.

A. B. Wylde. MODERN ABYSSINIA. With a Map and a Portrait. *Demy 8vo.* 15s. *net.*

G. Wyndham, M.P. THE POEMS OF WILLIAM SHAKESPEARE. With an Introduction and Notes. *Demy 8vo. Buck-ram, gilt top.* 10s. 6d.
'We have no hesitation in describing Mr. George Wyndham's introduction as a masterly piece of criticism, and all who love our Elizabethan literature will find a very garden of delight in it.'—*Spectator.*

R. Wyon and G. Prance. THE LAND OF THE BLACK MOUNTAIN. Being a description of Montenegro. With 40 Illustrations. *Crown 8vo.* 6s.

W. B. Yeats. AN ANTHOLOGY OF IRISH VERSE. *Revised and Enlarged Edition. Crown 8vo.* 3s. 6d.

T. M. Young. THE AMERICAN COTTON INDUSTRY: A Study of Work and Workers. With an Introduction by ELIJAH HELM, Secretary to the Manchester Chamber of Commerce. *Crown 8vo. Cloth,* 2s. 6d.; *paper boards,* 1s. 6d.
'Thorough, comprehensive, disconcert-ing.'—*St. James's Gazette.*
'Able and interesting; a really excellent contribution.'—*Pilot.*

Methuen's Standard Library

Crown 8vo. 6s. each Volume.

'A series which, by the beauty and excellence of production as well as by the qualifications of its editors, is one of the best things now to be found in the book market.'—*Manchester Guardian.*

MEMOIRS OF MY LIFE AND WRITINGS. By Edward Gibbon. Edited by G. Birkbeck Hill L.L.D.
THE DECLINE AND FALL OF THE ROMAN EMPIRE. By Edward Gibbon. Edited by J. B. Bury, LL.D. *In Seven Volumes. Also, Demy 8vo. Gilt top.* 8s. 6d. *each.*
THE NATURAL HISTORY OF SELBORNE. By Gilbert White. Edited by L. C. Miall, F.R.S., Assisted by W. Warde Fowler, M.A.
THE HISTORY OF THE LIFE OF THOMAS ELL-WOOD. Edited by C. G. Crump, M.A.
LA COMMEDIA DI DANTE ALIGHIERI. The Italian Text. Edited by Paget Toynbee, Litt.D., M.A. *Also, Demy 8vo. Gilt top.* 8s. 6d.
THE EARLY POEMS OF ALFRED, LORD TENNYSON Edited by J. Churton Collins, M.A.

IN MEMORIAM, MAUD, AND THE PRINCESS. By Alfred, Lord Tennyson. Edited by J. Churton Collins, M.A.
THE JOURNAL TO STELLA. By Jonathan Swift. Edited by G. A. Aitken, M.A.
THE LETTERS OF LORD CHESTERFIELD TO HIS SON. Edited by C. Strachey, and Notes by A. Calthrop. *Two Volumes.*
CRITICAL AND HISTORICAL ESSAYS. By Lord Mac-aulay. Edited by F.C. Montague, M.A. *Three Vols.*
THE FRENCH REVOLUTION. By Thomas Carlyle. Edited by C. R. L. Fletcher, Fellow of Magdalen College, Oxford. *Three Volumes.*
THE LIFE AND LETTERS OF OLIVER CROMWELL. By Thomas Carlyle. Edited by C. H. Firth, M.A., and Mrs. S. C. Lomas. *Three Volumes.*

Byzantine Texts

Edited by J. B. BURY, M.A., Litt.D.

ZACHARIAH OF MITYLENE. Translated by F. J. Hamilton, D.D., and E. W. Brooks. *Demy 8vo.* 12s. 6d. net.

EVAGRIUS. Edited by Léon Parmentier and M. Bidez. *Demy 8vo.* 10s. 6d. net.

THE HISTORY OF PSELLUS. Edited by C. Sathas. *Demy 8vo.* 15s. net.

ECTHESIS CHRONICA. Edited by Professor Lambros. *Demy 8vo.* 7s. 6d. net.

The Little Library

With Introductions, Notes, and Photogravure Frontispieces.

Pott 8vo. Each Volume, cloth, 1s. 6d. net ; leather, 2s. 6d. net.

'Altogether good to look upon, and to handle.'—*Outlook.*
'A perfect series.'—*Pilot.*
'It is difficult to conceive more attractive volumes.'—*St. James's Gazette.*
'Very delicious little books.'—*Literature.*

VANITY FAIR. By W. M. Thackeray. Edited by S. Gwynn. *Three Volumes.*
PENDENNIS. By W. M. Thackeray. Edited by S. Gwynn. *Three Volumes.*
ESMOND. By W. M. Thackeray. Edited by Stephen Gwynn. *Two Volumes.*
CHRISTMAS BOOKS. By W. M. Thackeray. Edited by Stephen Gwynn.
CHRISTMAS BOOKS. By Charles Dickens. Edited by Stephen Gwynn. *Two Volumes.*
SELECTIONS FROM GEORGE CRABBE. Edited by A. C. DEANE.
JOHN HALIFAX, GENTLEMAN. By Mrs. Craik. Edited by Annie Matheson. *Two Volumes.*
PRIDE AND PREJUDICE. By Jane Austen. Edited by E. V. Lucas. *Two Volumes.*
NORTHANGER ABBEY. By Jane Austen. Edited by E. V. Lucas.
THE PRINCESS. By Alfred, Lord Tennyson. Edited by Elizabeth Wordsworth.
MAUD. By Alfred, Lord Tennyson. Edited by Elizabeth Wordsworth.
IN MEMORIAM. By Alfred, Lord Tennyson. Edited by H. C. Beeching, M.A.
THE EARLY POEMS OF ALFRED, LORD TENNYSON. Edited by J. C. Collins, M.A.
A LITTLE BOOK OF ENGLISH LYRICS. With Notes.
THE INFERNO OF DANTE. Translated by H. F. Cary. Edited by Paget Toynbee, Litt.D., M.A.
THE PURGATORIO OF DANTE. Translated by H. F. Cary. Edited by Paget Toynbee, Litt.D., M.A.
THE PARADISO OF DANTE. Translated by H. F. Cary. Edited by Paget Toynbee, Litt.D., M.A.
A LITTLE BOOK OF SCOTTISH VERSE. Edited by T. F. Henderson.
A LITTLE BOOK OF LIGHT VERSE. Edited by A. C. Deane.
A LITTLE BOOK OF ENGLISH SONNETS. Edited by J. B. B. Nichols.

SELECTIONS FROM WORDSWORTH. Edited by Nowell C. Smith.
SELECTIONS FROM THE EARLY POEMS OF ROBERT BROWNING. Edited by W. Hall Griffin, M.A.
THE ENGLISH POEMS OF RICHARD CRASHAW. Edited by Edward Hutton.
SELECTIONS FROM WILLIAM BLAKE. Edited by M. Perugini.
A LITTLE BOOK OF LIFE AND DEATH. Edited by Mrs. Alfred Waterhouse.
A LITTLE BOOK OF ENGLISH PROSE. Edited by Mrs. P. A. Barnett.
EOTHEN. By A. W. Kinglake. With an Introduction and Notes.
CRANFORD. By Mrs. Gaskell. Edited by E. V. Lucas.
LAVENGRO. By George Borrow. Edited by F. Hindes Groome. *Two Volumes.*
ROMANY RYE. By George Borrow. Edited by John Sampson.
THE HISTORY OF THE CALIPH VATHEK. By William Beckford. Edited by E. Denison Ross.
THE COMPLEAT ANGLER. By Izaak Walton. Edited by J. Buchan.
MARRIAGE. By Susan Ferrier. Edited by Miss Goodrich-Freer and Lord Iddesleigh. *Two Volumes.*
THE INHERITANCE. By Susan Ferrier. Edited by Miss Goodrich-Freer and Lord Iddesleigh. *Two Volumes.*
ELIA, AND THE LAST ESSAYS OF ELIA. By Charles Lamb. Edited by E. V. Lucas.
A SENTIMENTAL JOURNEY. By Laurence Sterne. Edited by H. W. Paul.
MANSIE WAUCH. By D. M. Moir. Edited by T. F. Henderson.
THE INGOLDSBY LEGENDS. By R. H. Barham. Edited by J. B. Atlay. *Two Volumes.*
THE SCARLET LETTER. By Nathaniel Hawthorne. Edited by P. Dearmer.

The Little Guides

Pott 8vo, cloth, 3s.; leather, 3s. 6d. net.

OXFORD AND ITS COLLEGES. By J. Wells, M.A. Illustrated by E. H. New. *Fourth Edition.*
CAMBRIDGE AND ITS COLLEGES. By A. Hamilton Thompson. Illustrated by E. H. New.
THE MALVERN COUNTRY. By B. C. A. Windle, D.Sc., F.R.S. Illustrated by E. H. New.
SHAKESPEARE'S COUNTRY. By B. C. A. Windle, D.Sc., F.R.S. Illustrated by E. H. New. *Second Edition.*
SUSSEX. By F. G. Brabant, M.A. Illustrated by E. H. New.
WESTMINSTER ABBEY. By G. E. Troutbeck. Illustrated by F. D. Bedford.

NORFOLK. By W. A. Dutt. Illustrated by B. C. Boulter.
CORNWALL. By A. L. Salmon. Illustrated by B. C. Boulter.
BRITTANY. By S. Baring-Gould. Illustrated by J. Wylie.
THE ENGLISH LAKES. By F. G. Brabant, M.A. Illustrated by E. H. New. 4s. ; *leather, 4s. 6d. net.*
KENT. By G. Clinch. Illustrated by F. D. Bedford.
HERTFORDSHIRE. By H. W. Tompkins, F.R.H.S. Illustrated by E. H. New.
ROME. By C. G. Ellaby. Illustrated by B. C. Boulter.

Little Biographies

Fcap. 8vo.   Each volume, cloth, 3s. 6d. ; leather, 4s. net.

DANTE ALIGHIERI. By Paget Toynbee, Litt.D., M.A. With 12 Illustrations. *Second Edition.*

SAVONAROLA. By E. L. S. Horsburgh, M.A. With 12 Illustrations. *Second Edition.*

JOHN HOWARD. By E. C. S. Gibson, D.D., Vicar of Leeds. With 12 Illustrations.

TENNYSON. By A. C. Benson, M.A. With 12 Illustrations.

WALTER RALEIGH. By J. A. Taylor. With 12 Illustrations.

ERASMUS. By E. F. H. CAPEY. With 12 Illustrations.

THE YOUNG PRETENDER. By C. S. Terry. With 12 Illustrations.

ROBERT BURNS. By T. F. Henderson. With 12 Illustrations.

CHATHAM. By A. S. M'Dowall. With 12 Illustrations.

The Little Blue Books

General Editor, E. V. LUCAS.

Illustrated.   Demy 16mo.   2s. 6d.

'Very elegant and very interesting volumes.'—*Glasgow Herald.*
'A delightful series of diminutive volumes.'—*World.*
'The series should be a favourite among juveniles.'—*Observer.*
1. THE CASTAWAYS OF MEADOWBANK. By T. COBB.
2. THE BEECHNUT BOOK. By JACOB ABBOTT. Edited by E. V. LUCAS.
3. THE AIR GUN. By T. HILBERT.
4. A SCHOOL YEAR. By NETTA SYRETT.
5. THE PEELES AT THE CAPITAL. By T. HILBERT.
6. THE TREASURE OF PRINCEGATE PRIORY. By T. COBB.

The Illustrated Pocket Library of Plain and Coloured Books

Fcap. 8vo.   3s. 6d. net to 4s. 6d. net each volume.

A series, in small form, of some of the famous illustrated books of fiction and general literature. These will be faithfully reprinted from the first or best editions without introduction or notes.

THE LIFE AND DEATH OF JOHN MYTTON, ESQ. By Nimrod. With 18 Coloured Plates by Henry Alken and T. J. Rawlins. 3s. 6d. net. 100 copies on large Japanese paper, 21s. net.

THE TOUR OF DR. SYNTAX IN SEARCH OF THE PICTURESQUE. By William Combe. With 30 Coloured Plates by T. Rowlandson. 3s. 6d. net. 100 copies on large Japanese paper, 21s. net.

ILLUSTRATIONS OF THE BOOK OF JOB. Invented and engraved by William Blake. 3s. 6d. net.
These famous Illustrations—21 in number—are reproduced in photogravure. 100 copies are printed on large paper, with India proofs and a duplicate set of the plates. 15s. net.

THE HISTORY OF JOHNNY QUAE GENUS: the Little Foundling of the late Dr. Syntax. By the Author of 'The Three Tours.' With 24 Coloured Plates by Rowlandson. 3s. 6d. net. 100 copies on large Japanese paper. 21s. net.

WINDSOR CASTLE. By W. Harrison Ainsworth. With 22 Plates and 87 Woodcuts in the Text by George Cruikshank. 3s. 6d. net.

ÆSOP'S FABLES. With 380 Woodcuts by Thomas Bewick. 3s. 6d. net.

The following volumes, which are in active preparation, will be issued at short intervals, and as far as possible in the order given.

COLOURED BOOKS

THE VICAR OF WAKEFIELD. By Oliver Goldsmith. With 24 Coloured Plates by T. Rowlandson. 3s. 6d. net.
A reproduction of a very rare book.

HANDLEY CROSS. By R. S. Surtees. With 17 Coloured Plates and 100 Woodcuts in the Text by John Leech. 4s. 6d. net.

MR. SPONGE'S SPORTING TOUR. By R. S. Surtees. With 13 Coloured Plates and 90 Woodcuts in the Text by John Leech. 3s. 6d. net.

JORROCKS' JAUNTS AND JOLLITIES. By R. S. Surtees. With 15 Coloured Plates by H. Alken. 3s. 6d. net.
This volume is reprinted from the extremely rare and costly edition of 1843, which contains Alken's very fine illustrations instead of the usual ones by Phiz.

ASK MAMMA. By R. S. Surtees. With 13 Coloured Plates and 70 Woodcuts in the Text by John Leech. 3s. 6d. net.

THE TOUR OF DOCTOR SYNTAX IN SEARCH OF CONSOLATION. By William Combe. With 24 Coloured Plates by T. Rowlandson. 3s. 6d. net.

THE THIRD TOUR OF DOCTOR SYNTAX IN SEARCH OF A WIFE. By William Combe. With 24 Coloured Plates by T. Rowlandson. 3s. 6d. net.

THE ENGLISH DANCE OF DEATH, from the Designs of T. Rowlandson, with Metrical Illustrations by the Author of 'Doctor Syntax.' *Two Volumes.* 9s. net.
This book contains 76 Coloured Plates.

THE DANCE OF LIFE : A Poem. By the Author of 'Doctor Syntax.' Illustrated with 26 Coloured Engravings by T. Rowlandson. 4s. 6d. net.

THE LIFE OF A SPORTSMAN. By Nimrod. With 35 Coloured Plates by Henry Alken. 4s. 6d. net.

LIFE IN LONDON : or, the Day and Night Scenes of Jerry Hawthorn, Esq., and his Elegant Friend, Corinthian Tom. By Pierce Egan. With 36 Coloured Plates by I. R. and G. Cruikshank. With numerous Designs on Wood. 4s. 6d. net.

REAL LIFE IN LONDON : or, the Rambles and Adventures of Bob Tallyho, Esq., and his Cousin, The Hon. Tom Dashall. By an Amateur (Pierce Egan). With 31 Coloured Plates by Alken and Rowlandson, etc. *Two Volumes.* 9s. net.

LIFE IN PARIS: Comprising the Rambles, Sprees and Amours of Dick Wildfire, etc. By David Carey. With 21 Coloured Plates by George Cruikshank, and 22 Wood Engravings by the same Artist. *4s. 6d. net.*

REAL LIFE IN IRELAND: or, the Day and Night Scenes of Brian Boru, Esq., and his Elegant Friend, Sir Shawn O'Dogherty. By a Real Paddy. With 19 Coloured Plates by Heath, Marks, etc. *3s. 6d. net.*

THE LIFE OF AN ACTOR. By Pierce Egan. With 27 Coloured Plates by Theodore Lane, and several Designs on Wood. *4s. 6d. net.*

THE ENGLISH SPY. By Bernard Blackmantle. With 72 Coloured Plates by R. Cruikshank, and many Illustrations on Wood. *Two Volumes. 9s. net.*

THE ANALYSIS OF THE HUNTING FIELD. By R. S. Surtees. With 7 Coloured Plates by Henry Alken, and 43 Illustrations on Wood. *3s. 6d. net.*

THE MILITARY ADVENTURES OF JOHNNY NEWCOME. By an Officer. With 15 Coloured Plates by T. Rowlandson. *3s. 6d. net.*

THE ADVENTURES OF JOHNNY NEWCOME IN THE NAVY. With 16 Coloured Plates by T. Rowlandson. *3s. 6d. net.*

THE NATIONAL SPORTS OF GREAT BRITAIN. With Descriptions and 50 Coloured Plates by Henry Alken. *4s. 6d. net.*
This book is completely different from the large folio edition of ' National Sports' by the same artist, and none of the plates are similar.

PLAIN BOOKS

THE GRAVE: A Poem. By Robert Blair. Illustrated by 12 Etchings executed by Louis Schiavonetti from the Original Inventions of William Blake. With an Engraved Title Page and a Portrait of Blake by T. Phillips, R.A. *3s. 6d. net.*
The Illustrations are reproduced in photogravure. 100 copies are printed on Japanese paper, with India proofs and a duplicate set of the plates. *15s. net.*

THE TOWER OF LONDON. By W. Harrison Ainsworth. With 40 Plates and 58 Woodcuts in the Text by George Cruikshank. *3s. 6d. net.*

FRANK FAIRLEGH. By F. E. Smedley. With 30 Plates by George Cruikshank. *3s. 6d. net.*

HANDY ANDY. By Samuel Lover. With 24 Illustrations by the Author. *3s. 6d. net.*

THE COMPLEAT ANGLER. By Izaak Walton and Charles Cotton. With 14 Plates and 77 Woodcuts in the Text. *3s. 6d. net.*
This volume is reproduced from the beautiful edition of John Major of 1824.

THE PICKWICK PAPERS. By Charles Dickens. With the 43 Illustrations by Seymour and Phiz, the two Buss Plates and the 32 Contemporary Onwhyn Plates. *3s. 6d. net.*
This is a particularly interesting volume, containing, as it does, reproductions of very rare plates.

The Library of Devotion

With Introductions and (where necessary) Notes.

Pott 8vo, cloth, 2s. ; leather, 2s. 6d. net.

'This series is excellent.'—THE LATE BISHOP OF LONDON.
'Well worth the attention of the Clergy.'—THE BISHOP OF LICHFIELD.
'The new "Library of Devotion" is excellent.'—THE BISHOP OF PETERBOROUGH.
'Charming.'—*Record.*   'Delightful.'—*Church Bells.*

THE CONFESSIONS OF ST. AUGUSTINE. Edited by C. Bigg, D.D. *Third Edition.*

THE CHRISTIAN YEAR. Edited by Walter Lock, D.D. *Second Edition.*

THE IMITATION OF CHRIST. Edited by C. Bigg, D.D. *Second Edition.*

A BOOK OF DEVOTIONS. Edited by J. W. Stanbridge, B.D.

LYRA INNOCENTIUM. Edited by Walter Lock, D.D.

A SERIOUS CALL TO A DEVOUT AND HOLY LIFE. Edited by C. Bigg, D.D. *Second Edition.*

THE TEMPLE. Edited by E. C. S. Gibson, D.D.

A GUIDE TO ETERNITY. Edited by J. W. Stanbridge, B.D.

THE PSALMS OF DAVID. Edited by B. W. Randolph, D.D.

LYRA APOSTOLICA. Edited by Canon Scott Holland and Canon H. C. Beeching, M.A.

THE INNER WAY. Edited by A. W. Hutton, M.A.

THE THOUGHTS OF PASCAL. Edited by C. S. Jerram, M.A.

ON THE LOVE OF GOD. By St. Francis de Sales. Edited by W. J. Knox-Little, M.A.

A MANUAL OF CONSOLATION FROM THE SAINTS AND FATHERS. Edited by J. H. Burn, B.D

THE SONG OF SONGS. Edited by B. Blaxland, M.A.

THE DEVOTIONS OF ST. ANSELM. Edited by C. C. J. Webb, M.A.

GRACE ABOUNDING. By John Bunyan. Edited by S. C. Freer, M.A.

BISHOP WILSON'S SACRA PRIVATA. Edited by A. E. Burn, B.D.

LYRA SACRA: A Book of Sacred Verse. Selected and edited by H. C. Beeching, M.A., Canon of Westminster.

The Westminster Commentaries

General Editor, WALTER LOCK, D.D., Warden of Keble College,
Dean Ireland's Professor of Exegesis in the University of Oxford.

THE BOOK OF JOB. Edited by E. C. S. Gibson, D.D. *Demy 8vo. 6s.*

THE ACTS OF THE APOSTLES. Edited by R. B Rackham, M.A. *Demy 8vo. 12s. 6d.*

THE FIRST EPISTLE OF PAUL THE APOSTLE TO THE CORINTHIANS. Edited by H. L. Goudge, M.A. *Demy 8vo. 6s.*

Handbooks of Theology

THE XXXIX. ARTICLES OF THE CHURCH OF ENGLAND. Edited by E. C. S. Gibson, D.D. *Third and Cheaper Edition in One Volume. Demy 8vo. 12s. 6d.*

AN INTRODUCTION TO THE HISTORY OF RELIGION. By F. B. Jevons, M.A., Litt.D. *Second Edition. Demy 8vo. 10s. 6d.*

THE DOCTRINE OF THE INCARNATION. By R. L. Ottley, M.A. *Second and Cheaper Edition. Demy 8vo. 12s. 6d.*

AN INTRODUCTION TO THE HISTORY OF THE CREEDS. By A. E. Burn, B.D. *Demy 8vo.* 10s. 6d.

THE PHILOSOPHY OF RELIGION IN ENGLAND AND AMERICA. By Alfred Caldecott, D.D. *Demy 8vo.* 10s. 6d.

The Churchman's Library

General Editor, J. H. BURN, B.D., F.R.S.E., Examining Chaplain to the Bishop of Aberdeen.

THE BEGINNINGS OF ENGLISH CHRISTIANITY. By W. E. Collins, M.A. With Map. *Crown 8vo.* 3s. 6d.

SOME NEW TESTAMENT PROBLEMS. By Arthur Wright, M.A. *Crown 8vo.* 6s.

THE KINGDOM OF HEAVEN HERE AND HEREAFTER. By Canon Winterbotham, M.A., B.Sc., LL.B. *Crown 8vo.* 3s. 6d.

THE WORKMANSHIP OF THE PRAYER BOOK : Its Literary and Liturgical Aspects. By J. Dowden, D.D. *Second Edition. Crown 8vo.* 3s. 6d.

EVOLUTION. By F. B. Jevons, M.A., Litt.D. *Crown 8vo.* 3s. 6d.

THE OLD TESTAMENT AND THE NEW SCHOLARSHIP. By J. W. Peters, D.D. *Crown 8vo.* 6s.

THE CHURCHMAN'S INTRODUCTION TO THE OLD TESTAMENT. Edited by A. M. Mackay, B.A. *Crown 8vo.* 3s. 6d.

THE CHURCH OF CHRIST. By E. T. Green, M.A. *Crown 8vo.* 6s.

COMPARATIVE THEOLOGY. By J. A. MacCulloch. *Crown 8vo.* 6s.

The Churchman's Bible

General Editor, J. H. BURN, B.D., F.R.S.E.

The volumes are practical and devotional, and the text of the Authorised Version is explained in sections, which correspond as far as possible with the Church Lectionary.

THE EPISTLE TO THE GALATIANS. Edited by A. W. Robinson, M.A. *Fcap. 8vo.* 1s. 6d. *net.*

ECCLESIASTES. Edited by A. W. Streane, D.D. *Fcap. 8vo.* 1s. 6d. *net.*

THE EPISTLE TO THE PHILIPPIANS. Edited by C. R. D. Biggs, D.D. *Fcap. 8vo.* 1s. 6d. *net.*

THE EPISTLE OF ST. JAMES. Edited by H. W Fulford, M.A. *Fcap. 8vo.* 1s. 6d. *net.*

ISAIAH. Edited by W. E. Barnes, D.D., Hulsaean Professor of Divinity. *Two Volumes. Fcap. 8vo.* 2s. *net each.* Vol. I. With Map.

THE EPISTLE OF ST. PAUL THE APOSTLE TO THE EPHESIANS. Edited by G. H. Whitaker, M.A. *Fcap. 8vo.* 1s. 6d. *net.*

Leaders of Religion

Edited by H. C. BEECHING, M.A. *With Portraits. Crown 8vo.* 3s. 6d.

A series of short biographies of the most prominent leaders of religious life and thought of all ages and countries.

CARDINAL NEWMAN. By R. H. Hutton.
JOHN WESLEY. By J. H. Overton, M.A.
BISHOP WILBERFORCE. By G. W. Daniell, M.A.
CARDINAL MANNING. By A. W. Hutton, M.A.
CHARLES SIMEON. By H. C. G. Moule, D.D.
JOHN KEBLE. By Walter Lock, D.D.
THOMAS CHALMERS. By Mrs. Oliphant.
LANCELOT ANDREWES. By R. L. Ottley, M.A.
AUGUSTINE OF CANTERBURY. By E. L. Cutts, D.D.
WILLIAM LAUD. By W. H. Hutton, M.A.

JOHN KNOX. By F. MacCunn.
JOHN HOWE. By R. F. Horton, D.D.
BISHOP KEN. By F. A. Clarke, M.A.
GEORGE FOX, THE QUAKER. By T. Hodgkin. D.C.L.
JOHN DONNE. By Augustus Jessopp, D.D.
THOMAS CRANMER. By A. J. Mason.
BISHOP LATIMER. By R. M. Carlyle and A. J. Carlyle, M.A.
BISHOP BUTLER. By W. A. Spooner, M.A.

Social Questions of To=day
Edited by H. DE B. GIBBINS, Litt.D., M.A.
Crown 8vo. 2s. 6d.

TRADE UNIONISM—NEW AND OLD. By G. Howell. *Third Edition.*
THE CO-OPERATIVE MOVEMENT TO-DAY. By G. J. Holyoake. *Second Edition.*
PROBLEMS OF POVERTY. By J. A. Hobson, M.A. *Fourth Edition.*
THE COMMERCE OF NATIONS. By C. F. Bastable, M.A. *Second Edition.*
THE ALIEN INVASION. By W. H. Wilkins, B.A.
THE RURAL EXODUS. By P. Anderson Graham.
LAND NATIONALIZATION. By Harold Cox, B.A.
A SHORTER WORKING DAY. By H. de B. Gibbins and R. A. Hadfield.
BACK TO THE LAND: An Inquiry into Rural Depopulation. By H. E. Moore.
TRUSTS, POOLS, AND CORNERS. By J. Stephen Jeans.
THE FACTORY SYSTEM. By R. W. Cooke-Taylor.

THE STATE AND ITS CHILDREN. By Gertrude Tuckwell.
WOMEN'S WORK. By Lady Dilke, Miss Bulley, and Miss Whitley.
SOCIALISM AND MODERN THOUGHT. By M. Kauffmann.
THE HOUSING OF THE WORKING CLASSES. By E. Bowmaker.
THE PROBLEM OF THE UNEMPLOYED. By J. A. Hobson, M.A.
LIFE IN WEST LONDON. By Arthur Sherwell, M.A. *Third Edition.*
RAILWAY NATIONALIZATION. By Clement Edwards.
WORKHOUSES AND PAUPERISM. By Louisa Twining.
UNIVERSITY AND SOCIAL SETTLEMENTS. By W. Reason, M.A.

University Extension Series
Edited by J. E. SYMES, M.A.,
Principal of University College, Nottingham.
Crown 8vo. Price (with some exceptions) 2s. 6d.

A series of books on historical, literary, and scientific subjects, suitable for extension students and home-reading circles. Each volume is complete in itself, and the subjects are treated by competent writers in a broad and philosophic spirit.

THE INDUSTRIAL HISTORY OF ENGLAND. By H. de B. Gibbins, Litt.D., M.A. *Eighth Edition.* Revised. With Maps and Plans. 3s.
A HISTORY OF ENGLISH POLITICAL ECONOMY. By L. L. Price, M.A. *Third Edition.*
PROBLEMS OF POVERTY. By J. A. Hobson, M.A. *Fourth Edition.*
VICTORIAN POETS. By A. Sharp.
THE FRENCH REVOLUTION. By J. E. Symes, M.A.
PSYCHOLOGY. By F. S. Granger, M.A. *Second Edition.*
THE EVOLUTION OF PLANT LIFE: Lower Forms. By G. Massee. Illustrated.
AIR AND WATER. By V. B. Lewes, M.A. Illustrated.
THE CHEMISTRY OF LIFE AND HEALTH. By C. W. Kimmins, M.A. Illustrated.
THE MECHANICS OF DAILY LIFE. By V. P. Sells, M.A. Illustrated.
ENGLISH SOCIAL REFORMERS. By H. de B. Gibbins, Litt.D., M.A. *Second Edition.*
ENGLISH TRADE AND FINANCE IN THE SEVENTEENTH CENTURY. By W. A. S. Hewins, B.A.

THE CHEMISTRY OF FIRE. By M. M. Pattison Muir, M.A. Illustrated.
A TEXT-BOOK OF AGRICULTURAL BOTANY. By M. C. Potter, M.A., F.L.S. Illustrated. *Second Edition.* 4s. 6d.
THE VAULT OF HEAVEN. A Popular Introduction to Astronomy. By R. A. Gregory. With numerous Illustrations.
METEOROLOGY. By H. N. Dickson, F.R.S.E., F.R. Met. Soc. Illustrated.
A MANUAL OF ELECTRICAL SCIENCE. By George J. Burch, M.A., F.R.S. Illustrated. 3s.
THE EARTH. An Introduction to Physiography. By Evan Small, M.A. Illustrated.
INSECT LIFE. By F. W. Theobald, M.A. Illustrated.
ENGLISH POETRY FROM BLAKE TO BROWNING. By W. M. Dixon, M.A. *Second Edition.*
ENGLISH LOCAL GOVERNMENT. By E. Jenks, M.A.
THE GREEK VIEW OF LIFE. By G. L. Dickinson. *Second Edition.*

Methuen's Commercial Series
Edited by H. DE B. GIBBINS, Litt.D., M.A.
Crown 8vo.

COMMERCIAL EDUCATION IN THEORY AND PRACTICE. By E. E. Whitfield, M.A. 5s.
An introduction to Methuen's Commercial Series treating the question of Commercial Education fully from both the point of view of the teacher and of the parent.
BRITISH COMMERCE AND COLONIES FROM ELIZABETH TO VICTORIA. By H. de B. Gibbins, Litt.D., M.A. *Third Edition.* 2s.
COMMERCIAL EXAMINATION PAPERS. By H. de B. Gibbins, Litt.D., M.A. 1s. 6d.
THE ECONOMICS OF COMMERCE. By H. de B. Gibbins, Litt.D., M.A. 1s. 6d.
A GERMAN COMMERCIAL READER. By S. E. Bally, With Vocabulary. 2s.
A COMMERCIAL GEOGRAPHY OF THE BRITISH EMPIRE. By L. W. Lyde, M.A. *Third Edition.* 2s.

A PRIMER OF BUSINESS. By S. Jackson, M.A. *Third Edition.* 1s. 6d.
COMMERCIAL ARITHMETIC. By F. G. Taylor, M.A. *Third Edition.* 1s. 6d.
FRENCH COMMERCIAL CORRESPONDENCE. By S. E. Bally. With Vocabulary. *Third Edition.* 2s.
GERMAN COMMERCIAL CORRESPONDENCE. By S. E. Bally. With Vocabulary. *Second Edition.* 2s.
A FRENCH COMMERCIAL READER. By S. E. Bally. With Vocabulary. *Second Edition.* 2s.
PRECIS WRITING AND OFFICE CORRESPONDENCE. By E. E. Whitfield, M.A. *Second Edition.* 2s.
A GUIDE TO PROFESSIONS AND BUSINESS. By H. Jones. 1s. 6d.
THE PRINCIPLES OF BOOK-KEEPING BY DOUBLE ENTRY. By J. E. B. M'Allen, M.A. 2s.
COMMERCIAL LAW. By W. Douglas Edwards. 2s.
A COMMERCIAL GEOGRAPHY OF FOREIGN NATIONS. By F. C. Boon, B.A. 2s.

Classical Translations

Edited by H. F. Fox, M.A., Fellow and Tutor of Brasenose College, Oxford.

Crown 8vo.

ÆSCHYLUS—Agamemnon, Choephoroe, Eumenides. Translated by Lewis Campbell, LL.D. 5s.

CICERO—De Oratore I. Translated by E. N. P. Moor, M.A. 3s. 6d.

CICERO—Select Orations (Pro Milone, Pro Mureno, Philippic II., in Catilinam). Translated by H. E. D. Blakiston, M.A. 5s.

CICERO—De Natura Deorum. Translated by F. Brooks, M.A. 3s. 6d.

CICERO—De Officiis. Translated by G. B. Gardiner, M.A. 2s. 6d.

HORACE—The Odes and Epodes. Translated by A. Godley, M.A. 2s.

LUCIAN—Six Dialogues (Nigrinus, Icaro-Menippus, The Cock, The Ship, The Parasite, The Lover of Falsehood). Translated by S. T. Irwin, M.A. 3s. 6d.

SOPHOCLES—Electra and Ajax. Translated by E. D. A. Morshead, M.A. 2s. 6d.

TACITUS—Agricola and Germania. Translated by R. B. Townshend. 2s. 6d.

THE SATIRES OF JUVENAL. Translated by S. G. Owen. *Crown 8vo,* 2s. 6d.

Methuen's Junior School=Books

Edited by O. D. INSKIP, LL.D., and W. WILLIAMSON, B.A.

A CLASS-BOOK OF DICTATION PASSAGES. By W. Williamson, B.A. *Seventh Edition. Crown 8vo.* 1s. 6d.

THE GOSPEL ACCORDING TO ST. MARK. Edited by A. E. Rubie, M.A., Headmaster of the Royal Naval School, Eltham. With Three Maps. *Crown 8vo.* 1s. 6d.

A JUNIOR ENGLISH GRAMMAR. By W. Williamson, B.A. With numerous passages for parsing and analysis, and a chapter on Essay Writing. *Crown 8vo.* 2s.

A JUNIOR CHEMISTRY. By E. A. Tyler, B.A., F.C.S., Science Master at Framlingham College. With 73 Illustrations. *Crown 8vo.* 2s. 6d.

THE ACTS OF THE APOSTLES. Edited by A. E. Rubie, M.A., Headmaster Royal Naval School, Eltham. *Crown 8vo.* 2s.

A JUNIOR FRENCH GRAMMAR. By L. A. Sornet and M. J. Acatos, Modern Language Masters at King Edward's School, Birmingham.

School Examination Series

Edited by A. M. M. STEDMAN, M.A. *Crown 8vo.* 2s. 6d.

FRENCH EXAMINATION PAPERS. By A. M. M. Stedman, M.A. *Twelfth Edition.*
A KEY, issued to Tutors and Private Students only, to be had on application to the Publishers. *Fifth Edition. Crown 8vo.* 6s. net.

LATIN EXAMINATION PAPERS. By A. M. M. Stedman, M.A. *Eleventh Edition.*
KEY (*Fourth Edition*) issued as above. 6s. net.

GREEK EXAMINATION PAPERS. By A. M. M. Stedman, M.A. *Sixth Edition.*
KEY (*Second Edition*) issued as above. 6s. net.

GERMAN EXAMINATION PAPERS. By R. J. Morich. *Fifth Edition.*
KEY (*Second Edition*) issued as above. 6s. net.

HISTORY AND GEOGRAPHY EXAMINATION PAPERS. By C. H. Spence, M.A., Clifton College. *Second Edition.*

PHYSICS EXAMINATION PAPERS. By R. E. Steel, M.A., F.C.S.

GENERAL KNOWLEDGE EXAMINATION PAPERS. By A. M. M. Stedman, M.A. *Fourth Edition.*
KEY (*Second Edition*) issued as above. 7s. net.

EXAMINATION PAPERS IN ENGLISH HISTORY. By J. Tait Plowden-Wardlaw, B.A.

Junior Examination Series

Edited by A. M. M. STEDMAN, M.A. *Fcap. 8vo.* 1s.

JUNIOR FRENCH EXAMINATION PAPERS. By F. Jacob, B.A.

JUNIOR LATIN EXAMINATION PAPERS. By C. G. BOTTING, M.A.

JUNIOR ENGLISH EXAMINATION PAPERS. By W. Williamson, B.A.

JUNIOR ARITHMETIC EXAMINATION PAPERS. By W. S. Beard.

JUNIOR ALGEBRA EXAMINATION PAPERS. By W. S. Finn, M.A.

Technology—Textbooks of

Edited by PROFESSOR J. WERTHEIMER, F.I.C.

Fully Illustrated.

HOW TO MAKE A DRESS. By J. A. E. Wood. *Second Edition. Crown 8vo.* 1s. 6d.

CARPENTRY AND JOINERY. By F. C. Webber. *Third Edition. Crown 8vo.* 3s. 6d.

PRACTICAL MECHANICS. By Sidney H. Wells. *Second Edition. Crown 8vo.* 3s. 6d.

PRACTICAL PHYSICS. By H. Stroud, D.Sc., M.A. *Crown 8vo.* 3s. 6d.

MILLINERY, THEORETICAL AND PRACTICAL. By Clare Hill. *Crown 8vo.* 2s.

PRACTICAL CHEMISTRY. By W. French, M.A. *Crown 8vo.* Part I. *Second Edition.* 1s. 6d.

TECHNICAL ARITHMETIC AND GEOMETRY. By C. T. Millis, M.I.M.E. With Diagrams. *Crown 8vo.* 3s. 6d.

PART II.—FICTION

Marie Corelli's Novels.
Crown 8vo. 6s. each.

A ROMANCE OF TWO WORLDS. *Twenty-Fourth Edition.*
VENDETTA. *Nineteenth Edition.*
THELMA. *Twenty-Ninth Edition.*
ARDATH: THE STORY OF A DEAD SELF. *Fourteenth Edition.*
THE SOUL OF LILITH. *Twelfth Edit.*
WORMWOOD. *Thirteenth Edition.*
BARABBAS: A DREAM OF THE WORLD'S TRAGEDY. *Thirty-Eighth Edition.*
 'The tender reverence of the treatment and the imaginative beauty of the writing have reconciled us to the daring of the conception. This "Dream of the World's Tragedy" is a lofty and not inadequate paraphrase of the supreme climax of the inspired narrative.'—*Dublin Review.*
THE SORROWS OF SATAN. *Forty-Sixth Edition.*
 'A very powerful piece of work. . . . The conception is magnificent, and is likely to win an abiding place within the memory of man. . . . The author has immense command of language, and a limitless audacity. . . . This interesting and remarkable romance will live long after much of the ephemeral literature of the day is forgotten. . . . A literary phenomenon . . . novel, and even sublime.'—W. T. STEAD in the *Review of Reviews.*
THE MASTER CHRISTIAN.
 [*165th Thousand.*
 'It cannot be denied that "The Master Christian" is a powerful book; that it is one likely to raise uncomfortable questions in all but the most self-satisfied readers, and that it strikes at the root of the failure of the Churches—the decay of faith—in a manner which shows the inevitable disaster heaping up. . . . The good Cardinal Bonpré is a beautiful figure, fit to stand beside the good Bishop in "Les Misérables." It is a book with a serious purpose expressed with absolute unconventionality and passion . . . And this is to say it is a book worth reading.'—*Examiner.*
TEMPORAL POWER: A STUDY IN SUPREMACY.
 [*150th Thousand.*
 'It is impossible to read such a work as "Temporal Power" without becoming convinced that the story is intended to convey certain criticisms on the ways of the world and certain suggestions for the betterment of humanity. . . . The chief characteristics of the book are an attack on conventional prejudices and manners and on certain practices attributed to the Roman Church (the policy of M. Combes makes parts of the novel specially up to date), and the propounding of theories for the improvement of the social and political systems. . . . If the chief intention of the book was to hold the mirror up to shams, injustice, dishonesty, cruelty, and neglect of conscience, nothing but praise can be given to that intention.'—*Morning Post.*

Anthony Hope's Novels.
Crown 8vo. 6s. each.

THE GOD IN THE CAR. *Ninth Edition.*
 'A very remarkable book, deserving of critical analysis impossible within our limit; brilliant, but not superficial; well considered, but not elaborated; constructed with the proverbial art that conceals, but yet allows itself to be enjoyed by readers to whom fine literary method is a keen pleasure.'—*The World.*

A CHANGE OF AIR. *Sixth Edition.*
 'A graceful, vivacious comedy, true to human nature. The characters are traced with a masterly hand.'—*Times.*

A MAN OF MARK. *Fifth Edition.*
 'Of all Mr. Hope's books, "A Man of Mark" is the one which best compares with "The Prisoner of Zenda."'—*National Observer.*

THE CHRONICLES OF COUNT ANTONIO. *Fifth Edition.*
 'It is a perfectly enchanting story of love and chivalry, and pure romance. The Count is the most constant, desperate, and modest and tender of lovers, a peerless gentleman, an intrepid fighter, a faithful friend, and a magnanimous foe.'—*Guardian.*
PHROSO. Illustrated by H. R. MILLAR. *Sixth Edition.*
 'The tale is thoroughly fresh, quick with vitality, stirring the blood.'—*St. James's Gazette.*
SIMON DALE. Illustrated. *Sixth Edition.*
 'There is searching analysis of human nature, with a most ingeniously constructed plot. Mr. Hope has drawn the contrasts of his women with marvellous subtlety and delicacy.'—*Times.*
THE KING'S MIRROR. *Fourth Edition.*
 'In elegance, delicacy, and tact it ranks with the best of his novels, while in the wide range of its portraiture and the subtilty of its analysis it surpasses all his earlier ventures.'—*Spectator.*
QUISANTE. *Fourth Edition.*
 'The book is notable for a very high literary quality, and an impress of power and mastery on every page.'—*Daily Chronicle.*

W. W. Jacobs' Novels.

Crown 8vo.   3s. 6d. each.

MANY CARGOES. *Twenty-Seventh Edition.*
SEA URCHINS. *Tenth Edition.*
A MASTER OF CRAFT. Illustrated. *Sixth Edition.*
    'Can be unreservedly recommended to all who have not lost their appetite for wholesome laughter.'—*Spectator.*
    'The best humorous book published for many a day.'—*Black and White.*

LIGHT FREIGHTS. Illustrated. *Fourth Edition.*
    'His wit and humour are perfectly irresistible. Mr. Jacobs writes of skippers, and mates, and seamen, and his crew are the jolliest lot that ever sailed.'—*Daily News.*
    'Laughter in every page.'—*Daily Mail.*

Lucas Malet's Novels.

Crown 8vo.   6s. each.

COLONEL ENDERBY'S WIFE. *Third Edition.*
A COUNSEL OF PERFECTION. *New Edition.*
LITTLE PETER. *Second Edition.* 3s. 6d.
THE WAGES OF SIN. *Thirteenth Edition.*
THE CARISSIMA. *Fourth Edition.*
THE GATELESS BARRIER. *Fourth Edition.*
    'In "The Gateless Barrier" it is at once evident that, whilst Lucas Malet has preserved her birthright of originality, the artistry, the actual writing, is above even the high level of the books that were born before.'—*Westminster Gazette.*

THE HISTORY OF SIR RICHARD CALMADY. *Seventh Edition.* A Limited Edition in Two Volumes. *Crown 8vo.* 12s.
    'A picture finely and amply conceived. In the strength and insight in which the story has been conceived, in the wealth of fancy and reflection bestowed upon its execution, and in the moving sincerity of its pathos throughout, "Sir Richard Calmady" must rank as the great novel of a great writer.'—*Literature.*
    'The ripest fruit of Lucas Malet's genius. A picture of maternal love by turns tender and terrible.'—*Spectator.*
    'A remarkably fine book, with a noble motive and a sound conclusion.'—*Pilot.*

Gilbert Parker's Novels.

Crown 8vo.   6s. each.

PIERRE AND HIS PEOPLE. *Fifth Edition.*
    'Stories happily conceived and finely executed. There is strength and genius in Mr. Parker's style.'—*Daily Telegraph.*
MRS. FALCHION. *Fourth Edition.*
    'A splendid study of character.'—*Athenæum.*
THE TRANSLATION OF A SAVAGE. *Second Edition.*
THE TRAIL OF THE SWORD. Illustrated. *Seventh Edition.*
    'A rousing and dramatic tale. A book like this is a joy inexpressible.'—*Daily Chronicle.*
WHEN VALMOND CAME TO PONTIAC: The Story of a Lost Napoleon. *Fifth Edition.*
    'Here we find romance—real, breathing, living romance. The character of Valmond is drawn unerringly.'—*Pall Mall Gazette.*

AN ADVENTURER OF THE NORTH: The Last Adventures of 'Pretty Pierre.' *Third Edition.*
    'The present book is full of fine and moving stories of the great North.'—*Glasgow Herald.*
THE SEATS OF THE MIGHTY. Illustrated. *Twelfth Edition.*
    'Mr. Parker has produced a really fine historical novel.'—*Athenæum.*
    'A great book.'—*Black and White.*
THE BATTLE OF THE STRONG: a Romance of Two Kingdoms. Illustrated. *Fourth Edition.*
    'Nothing more vigorous or more human has come from Mr. Gilbert Parker than this novel.'—*Literature.*
THE POMP OF THE LAVILETTES. *Second Edition.* 3s. 6d.
    'Unforced pathos, and a deeper knowledge of human nature than he has displayed before.'—*Pall Mall Gazette.*

Arthur Morrison's Novels.

Crown 8vo. 6s. each.

TALES OF MEAN STREETS. *Fifth Edition.*
'A great book. The author's method is amazingly effective, and produces a thrilling sense of reality. The writer lays upon us a master hand. The book is simply appalling and irresistible in its interest. It is humorous also; without humour it would not make the mark it is certain to make.'—*World.*

A CHILD OF THE JAGO. *Fourth Edition.*
'The book is a masterpiece.'—*Pall Mall Gazette.*

TO LONDON TOWN. *Second Edition.*
'This is the new Mr. Arthur Morrison, gracious and tender, sympathetic and human.'—*Daily Telegraph.*

CUNNING MURRELL.
'Admirable. . . . Delightful humorous relief . . . a most artistic and satisfactory achievement.'—*Spectator.*

THE HOLE IN THE WALL. *Third Edition.*
'A masterpiece of artistic realism. It has a finality of touch that only a master may command.'—*Daily Chronicle.*
'An absolute masterpiece, which any novelist might be proud to claim.'—*Graphic.*
' "The Hole in the Wall" is a masterly piece of work. His characters are drawn with amazing skill. Extraordinary power.'—*Daily Telegraph.*

Eden Phillpotts' Novels.

Crown 8vo. 6s. each.

LYING PROPHETS.
CHILDREN OF THE MIST. *Fifth Edition.*
THE HUMAN BOY. With a Frontispiece. *Fourth Edition.*
'Mr. Phillpotts knows exactly what school-boys do, and can lay bare their in-most thoughts; likewise he shows an all-pervading sense of humour.'—*Academy.*
SONS OF THE MORNING. *Second Edition.*
'A book of strange power and fascination.'—*Morning Post.*
THE STRIKING HOURS. *Second Edition.*
'Tragedy and comedy, pathos and humour, are blended to a nicety in this volume.'—*World.*
'The whole book is redolent of a fresher and ampler air than breathes in the circum-scribed life of great towns.'—*Spectator.*

FANCY FREE. Illustrated. *Second Edition.*
'Of variety and racy humour there is plenty.'—*Daily Graphic.*

THE RIVER. *Third Edition.*
' "The River" places Mr. Phillpotts in the front rank of living novelists.'—*Punch.*
'Since "Lorna Doone" we have had nothing so picturesque as this new romance.' *Birmingham Gazette.*
'Mr. Phillpotts's new book is a master-piece which brings him indisputably into the front rank of English novelists.'—*Pall Mall Gazette.*
'This great romance of the River Dart. The finest book Mr. Eden Phillpotts has written.'—*Morning Post.*

S. Baring-Gould's Novels.

Crown 8vo. 6s. each.

ARMINELL. *Fifth Edition.*
URITH. *Fifth Edition.*
IN THE ROAR OF THE SEA. *Seventh Edition.*
MRS. CURGENVEN OF CURGENVEN. *Fourth Edition.*
CHEAP JACK ZITA. *Fourth Edition.*
THE QUEEN OF LOVE. *Fifth Edition.*
MARGERY OF QUETHER. *Third Edition.*
JACQUETTA. *Third Edition.*
KITTY ALONE. *Fifth Edition.*
NOÉMI. Illustrated. *Fourth Edition.*
THE BROOM-SQUIRE. Illustrated. *Fourth Edition.*

THE PENNYCOMEQUICKS. *Third Edition.*
DARTMOOR IDYLLS.
GUAVAS THE TINNER. Illustrated. *Second Edition.*
BLADYS. Illustrated. *Second Edition.*
DOMITIA. Illustrated. *Second Edition.*
PABO THE PRIEST.
WINIFRED. Illustrated. *Second Edition.*
THE FROBISHERS.
ROYAL GEORGIE. Illustrated.
MISS QUILLET. Illustrated.
LITTLE TU'PENNY. *A New Edition.* 6d.

Robert Barr's Novels.
Crown 8vo. 6s. each.

IN THE MIDST OF ALARMS. *Third Edition.*
'A book which has abundantly satisfied us by its capital humour.'—*Daily Chronicle.*
THE MUTABLE MANY. *Second Edition.*
'There is much insight in it, and much excellent humour.'—*Daily Chronicle.*
THE COUNTESS TEKLA. *Third Edition.*
'Of these mediæval romances, which are now gaining ground "The Countess Tekla" is the very best we have seen.'—*Pall Mall Gazette.*

THE STRONG ARM. Illustrated. *Second Edition.*

THE VICTORS.
'Mr. Barr has a rich sense of humour.'—*Onlooker.*
'A very convincing study of American life in its business and political aspects.'—*Pilot.*
'Good writing, illuminating sketches of character, and constant variety of scene and incident.'—*Times.*

J. H. M. Abbot, Author of 'Tommy Cornstalk.' PLAIN AND VELDT. *Crown 8vo. 6s.*

F. Anstey, Author of 'Vice Versa. A BAYARD FROM BENGAL. Illustrated by BERNARD PARTRIDGE. *Third Edition. Crown 8vo. 3s. 6d.*
'A highly amusing story.'—
Pall Mall Gazette.
'A volume of rollicking irresponsible fun.'—
Outlook.
'This eminently mirthful narrative.'—
Globe.
'Immensely diverting.'—*Glasgow Herald.*
Richard Bagot. A ROMAN MYSTERY. *Third Edition. Crown 8vo. 6s.*
'An admirable story. The plot is sensational and original, and the book is full of telling situations.'—*St. James's Gazette.*
Andrew Balfour. BY STROKE OF SWORD. Illustrated. *Fourth Edition. Crown 8vo. 6s.*
'A recital of thrilling interest, told with unflagging vigour.'—*Globe.*
VENGEANCE IS MINE. Illustrated. *Crown 8vo. 6s.*
See also Fleur de Lis Novels.
M. C. Balfour. THE FALL OF THE SPARROW. *Crown 8vo. 6s.*
S. Baring Gould. See page 30.
Jane Barlow. THE LAND OF THE SHAMROCK. *Crown 8vo. 6s.*
FROM THE EAST UNTO THE WEST. *Crown 8vo. 6s.*
THE FOUNDING OF FORTUNES. *Crown 8vo. 6s.*
'This interesting and delightful book. Its author has done nothing better, and it is scarcely an exaggeration to say that it would be an injustice to Ireland not to read it.'—*Scotsman.*
See also Fleur de Lis Novels.
Robert Barr. See page 32.
J. A. Barry. IN THE GREAT DEEP. *Crown 8vo. 6s.*
George Bartram, Author of 'The People of Clopton.' THE THIRTEEN EVENINGS. *Crown 8vo. 6s.*

Harold Begbie. THE ADVENTURES OF SIR JOHN SPARROW. *Crown 8vo. 6s.*
'Mr. Begbie often recalls Stevenson's manner and makes "Sir John Sparrow" most diverting writing. Sir John is inspired with the idea that it is his duty to reform the world, and launches into the vortex of faddists. His experiences are traced with spacious and Rabelaisian humour. Every character has the salience of a type. Entertainingly and deftly written.'—
Daily Graphic.
E. F. Benson. DODO: A Detail of the Day. *Crown 8vo. 6s.*
THE CAPSINA. *Crown 8vo. 6s.*
See also Fleur de Lis Novels.
Margaret Benson. SUBJECT TO VANITY. *Crown 8vo. 3s. 6d.*
Sir Walter Besant. A FIVE YEARS' TRYST, and Other Stories. *Crown 8vo. 6s.*
Mrs. E. Bland (E. Nesbit). THE RED HOUSE. Illustrated. *Crown 8vo. 6s.*
C. Stewart Bowles. A STRETCH OFF THE LAND. *Crown 8vo. 6s.*
Emma Brooke. THE POET'S CHILD. *Crown 8vo. 6s.*
Shan. F. Bullock. THE SQUIREEN. *Crown 8vo. 6s.*
J. Bloundelle Burton, Author of 'The Clash of Arms.' THE YEAR ONE: A Page of the French Revolution. Illustrated. *Crown 8vo. 6s.*
DENOUNCED. *Crown 8vo. 6s.*
THE CLASH OF ARMS. *Crown 8vo. 6s.*
ACROSS THE SALT SEAS. *Crown 8vo. 6s.*
SERVANTS OF SIN. *Crown 8vo. 6s.*
THE FATE OF VALSEC. *Crown 8vo. 6s.*
'The characters are admirably portrayed. The book not only arrests and sustains the attention, but conveys valuable information in the most pleasant guise.'—*Morning Post.*
A BRANDED NAME. *Crown 8vo. 6s.*
See also Fleur de Lis Novels.
Ada Cambridge. THE DEVASTATORS. *Crown 8vo. 6s.*
PATH AND GOAL. *Crown 8vo. 6s.*

Bernard Capes, Author of 'The Lake of Wine. PLOTS. *Crown 8vo. 6s.*
'The stories are excellently fanciful and concentrated and quite worthy of the author's best work.'—*Morning Leader.*

Weatherby Chesney. JOHN TOPP: PIRATE. *Second Edition. Crown 8vo. 6s.*
THE FOUNDERED GALLEON. *Crown 8vo. 6s.*
THE BRANDED PRINCE. *Crown 8vo. 6s.*
'Always highly interesting and surprising.'—*Daily Express.*
'An ingenious, cleverly-contrived story.'— *Outlook.*

Mrs. W. K. Clifford. A WOMAN ALONE. *Crown 8vo. 3s. 6d.*
See also Fleur de Lis Novels.

Hugh Clifford. A FREE LANCE OF TO-DAY. *Crown 8vo. 6s.*

J. Maclaren Cobban. THE KING OF ANDAMAN: A Saviour of Society. *Crown 8vo. 6s.*
WILT THOU HAVE THIS WOMAN? *Crown 8vo. 6s.*
THE ANGEL OF THE COVENANT. *Crown 8vo. 6s.*

E. H. Cooper, Author of 'Mr. Blake of Newmarket.' A FOOL'S YEAR. *Crown 8vo. 6s.*

Julian Corbett. A BUSINESS IN GREAT WATERS. *Crown 8vo. 6s.*

Marie Corelli. See page 28.

L. Cope Cornford. CAPTAIN JACOBUS: A Romance of the Road. *Cr. 8vo. 6s.*
See also Fleur de Lis Novels.

Stephen Crane. WOUNDS IN THE RAIN. *Crown 8vo. 6s.*

S. R. Crockett, Author of 'The Raiders,' etc. LOCHINVAR. Illustrated. *Second Edition. Crown 8vo. 6s.*
'Full of gallantry and pathos, of the clash of arms, and brightened by episodes of humour and love.'—*Westminster Gazette.*
THE STANDARD BEARER. *Cr. 8vo. 6s.*
'Mr. Crockett at his best.'—*Literature.*

B. M. Croker, Author of 'Peggy of the Bartons.' ANGEL. *Third Edition. Crown 8vo. 6s.*
'An excellent story. Clever pictures of Anglo-Indian life abound. The heroine is delightful.'—*Manchester Guardian.*
PEGGY OF THE BARTONS. *Crown 8vo. 6s.*
A STATE SECRET. *Crown 8vo. 3s. 6d.*

Hope Dawlish. A SECRETARY OF LEGATION. *Crown 8vo. 6s.*

C. E. Denny. THE ROMANCE OF UPFOLD MANOR. *Crown 8vo. 6s.*

Evelyn Dickinson. A VICAR'S WIFE. *Crown 8vo. 6s.*
THE SIN OF ANGELS. *Crown 8vo. 3s. 6d.*

Harris Dickson. THE BLACK WOLF'S BREED. Illustrated. *Second Edition. Crown 8vo. 6s.*

A. Conan Doyle, Author of 'Sherlock Holmes,' 'The White Company,' etc. ROUND THE RED LAMP. *Eighth Edition. Crown 8vo. 6s.*
'The book is far and away the best view that has been vouchsafed us behind the scenes of the consulting-room.'—*Illustrated London News.*

Sara Jeannette Duncan (Mrs. Everard Cotes), Author of 'A Voyage of Consolation.' THOSE DELIGHTFUL AMERICANS. Illustrated. *Third Edition. Crown 8vo. 6s.*
'A rattling picture of American life, bright and good-tempered throughout.'— *Scotsman.*
THE PATH OF A STAR. Illustrated. *Second Edition. Crown 8vo. 6s.*
See also Fleur de Lis Novels.

C. F. Embree. A HEART OF FLAME. *Crown 8vo. 6s.*

G. Manville Fenn. AN ELECTRIC SPARK. *Crown 8vo. 6s.*
ELI'S CHILDREN. *Crown 8vo. 2s. 6d.*
A DOUBLE KNOT. *Crown 8vo. 2s. 6d.*
See also Fleur de Lis Novels.

J. H. Findlater. THE GREEN GRAVES OF BALGOWRIE. *Fourth Edition. Crown 8vo. 6s.*
'A powerful and vivid story.'—*Standard.*
'A beautiful story, sad and strange as truth itself.'—*Vanity Fair.*
'A singularly original, clever, and beautiful story.'—*Guardian.*
A DAUGHTER OF STRIFE. *Crown 8vo. 6s.*
See also Fleur de Lis Novels.

Mary Findlater. OVER THE HILLS. *Second Edition. Crown 8vo. 6s.*
BETTY MUSGRAVE. *Second Edition. Crown 8vo. 6s.*
A NARROW WAY. *Third Edition. Crown 8vo. 6s.*

J. S. Fletcher. THE BUILDERS. *Crown 8vo. 6s.*
See also Fleur de Lis Novels.

R. E. Forrest. THE SWORD OF AZRAEL, a Chronicle of the Great Mutiny. *Crown 8vo. 6s.*

M. E. Francis. MISS ERIN. *Second Edition. Crown 8vo. 6s.*

Tom Gallon, Author of 'Kiddy.' RICKERBY'S FOLLY. *Crown 8vo. 6s.*

Mary Gaunt. DEADMAN'S. *Crown 8vo. 6s.*
THE MOVING FINGER. *Crown 8vo. 3s. 6d.*
See also Fleur de Lis Novels.

Dorothea Gerard, Author of 'Lady Baby.' THE MILLION. *Crown 8vo. 6s.*
THE CONQUEST OF LONDON. *Second Edition. Crown 8vo. 6s.*

THE SUPREME CRIME. *Cr. 8vo.* 6s.
HOLY MATRIMONY. *Second Edition.*
Crown 8vo. 6s.
'The love story which it enshrines is a
very pretty and tender one.'—*Morning
Leader.*
'Distinctly interesting.'—*Athenæum.*
THINGS THAT HAVE HAPPENED.
Crown 8vo. 6s.

R. Murray Gilchrist. WILLOWBRAKE.
Crown 8vo. 6s.

Algernon Gissing. THE KEYS OF THE
HOUSE. *Crown 8vo.* 6s.

George Gissing, Author of 'Demos,' 'In the
Year of Jubilee,' etc.   THE TOWN
TRAVELLER. *Second Edition. Crown
8vo.* 6s.
THE CROWN OF LIFE. *Crown 8vo.* 6s.

Ernest Glanville. THE KLOOF BRIDE.
Crown 8vo. 3s. 6d.
THE LOST REGIMENT. *Crown 8vo.*
3s. 6d.
THE DESPATCH RIDER. *Crown 8vo.*
3s. 6d.
THE INCA'S TREASURE. Illustrated.
Crown 8vo. 3s. 6d.
'No lack of exciting incident.'—*Scotsman.*
'Most thrilling and exciting.'—
Glasgow Herald.

Charles Gleig. BUNTER'S CRUISE.
Illustrated. *Crown 8vo.* 3s. 6d.

Julien Gordon. MRS. CLYDE. *Crown
8vo.* 6s.
'A clever picture of many phases of
feminine and American life.'—
Daily Express.
'Full of vivacity, with many excruciatingly
clever and entertaining scenes.'—*Pilot.*
WORLD'S PEOPLE. *Crown 8vo.* 6s.

S. Gordon. A HANDFUL OF EXOTICS.
Crown 8vo. 3s. 6d.

C. F. Goss. THE REDEMPTION OF
DAVID CORSON. *Third Edition.*
Crown 8vo. 6s.

E. M'Queen Gray. ELSA. *Crown 8vo.* 6s.
MY STEWARDSHIP. *Crown 8vo.* 2s. 6d.

A. G. Hales. JAIR THE APOSTATE.
Illustrated. *Crown 8vo.* 6s.
'An extraordinarily vivid story.'—*World.*
'Mr. Hales has a vivid pen, and the
scenes are described with vigour and colour.'—
Morning Post.

Lord Ernest Hamilton. MARY HAMIL-
TON. *Third Edition. Crown 8vo.* 6s.

Mrs. Burton Harrison. A PRINCESS
OF THE HILLS. Illustrated. *Crown 8vo.*
6s.
'Vigorous, swift, exciting.'—*Outlook.*
'A singularly pleasant story of the Tyrol.'—
Morning Post.

Robert Hichens, Author of 'Flames,'
etc. THE PROPHET OF BERKELEY
SQUARE. *Second Edition. Crown 8vo.*
6s.

'One continuous sparkle. Mr. Hichens
is witty, satirical, caustic, irresistibly hum-
orous.'—*Birmingham Gazette.*
TONGUES OF CONSCIENCE. *Second
Edition. Crown 8vo.* 6s.
FELIX. *Fourth Edition. Crown 8vo.* 6s.
'Firm in texture, sane, sincere, and
natural. "Felix" is a clever book, and in
many respects a true one.'—*Daily Chronicle.*
'A really powerful book.'—
Morning Leader.
'The story is related with unflagging
spirit.'—*World.*
'"Felix" will undoubtedly add to a con-
siderable reputation.'—*Daily Mail.*
See also Fleur de Lis Novels.

John Oliver Hobbes, Author of 'Robert
Orange.' THE SERIOUS WOOING.
Crown 8vo. 6s.
'Mrs. Craigie is as brilliant as she ever
has been ; her characters are all illuminated
with sparkling gems of description, and the
conversation scintillates with an almost
bewildering blaze.'—*Athenæum.*

Anthony Hope. See page 28.

I. Hooper. THE SINGER OF MARLY.
Crown 8vo. 6s.

Violet Hunt. THE HUMAN IN-
TEREST. *Crown 8vo.* 6s.

C. J. Cutcliffe Hyne, Author of 'Captain
Kettle.' PRINCE RUPERT THE
BUCCANEER. With 8 Illustrations.
Second Edition. Crown 8vo. 6s.
MR. HORROCKS, PURSER. *Crown
8vo.* 6s.

W. W. Jacobs. See page 29.

Henry James, Author of 'What Maisie
Knew.' THE SACRED FOUNT.
Crown 8vo. 6s.
THE SOFT SIDE. *Second Edition.*
Crown 8vo. 6s.
THE BETTER SORT. *Crown 8vo.* 6s.

Gustaf Janson. ABRAHAM'S SACRI-
FICE. *Crown 8vo.* 6s.

C. F. Keary. THE JOURNALIST.
Crown 8vo. 6s.

Florence Finch Kelly. WITH HOOPS
OF STEEL. *Crown 8vo.* 6s.

Hon. Emily Lawless. TRAITS AND
CONFIDENCES. *Crown 8vo.* 6s.
WITH ESSEX IN IRELAND. *New
Edition. Crown 8vo.* 6s.
See also Fleur de Lis Novels.

Harry Lawson, Author of 'When the Billy
Boils.' CHILDREN OF THE BUSH.
Crown 8vo. 6s.
'Full of human sympathy and the genuine
flavour of a wild, untrammelled, unsophisti-
cated life.'—*Morning Leader.*
'The author writes of the wild, picturesque
life "out back," with all the affection of a
native and the penetrating insight of long
observation.'—*Daily Telegraph.*

E. Lynn Linton. THE TRUE HISTORY OF JOSHUA DAVIDSON, Christian and Communist. *Eleventh Edition. Crown 8vo. 1s.*

Norma Lorimer. MIRRY ANN. *Crown 8vo. 6s.*
JOSIAH'S WIFE. *Crown 8vo. 6s.*

Cecil Lowis. THE MACHINATIONS OF THE MYO-OK. *Crown 8vo. 6s.*

Charles K. Lush. THE AUTOCRATS. *Crown 8vo. 6s.*

Edna Lyall. DERRICK VAUGHAN, NOVELIST. *42nd thousand. Crown 8vo. 3s. 6d.*

S. Macnaughtan. THE FORTUNE OF CHRISTINA MACNAB. *Second Edition. Crown 8vo. 6s.*

A. Macdonell. THE STORY OF TERESA. *Crown 8vo. 6s.*

Harold Macgrath. THE PUPPET CROWN. Illustrated. *Crown 8vo. 6s.*

G. Makgill. OUTSIDE AND OVERSEAS. *Crown 8vo. 6s.*

Lucas Malet. See page 29.

Mrs. M. E. Mann. OLIVIA'S SUMMER. *Second Edition. Crown 8vo. 6s.*
'An exceptionally clever book, told with consummate artistry and reticence.'—*Daily Mail.*
'Full of shrewd insight and quiet humour.—*Academy.*
'Wholly delightful; a very beautiful and refreshing tale.'—*Pall Mall Gazette.*
'The author touches nothing that she does not adorn, so delicate and firm is her hold.'—*Manchester Guardian.*
'A powerful story.'—*Times.*
A LOST ESTATE. *A New Edition. Crown 8vo. 6s.*
THE PARISH OF HILBY. *A New Edition. Crown 8vo. 6s.*

Richard Marsh. BOTH SIDES OF THE VEIL. *Second Edition. Crown 8vo. 6s.*
THE SEEN AND THE UNSEEN. *Crown 8vo. 6s.*
MARVELS AND MYSTERIES. *Crown 8vo. 6s.*
THE TWICKENHAM PEERAGE. *Second Edition. Crown 8vo. 6s.*
'It is a long time since my Baronite read a novel of such entrancing interest as 'The Twickenham Peerage.' He recommends the gentle reader to get the book. In addition to its breathless interest, it is full of character and bubbling with fun.'—*Punch.*

A. E. W. Mason, Author of 'The Courtship of Morrice Buckler,' 'Miranda of the Balcony,' etc. CLEMENTINA. Illustrated. *Crown 8vo. 6s.*
'A romance of the most delicate ingenuity and humour . . . the very quintessence of romance.'—*Spectator.*

Helen Mathers, Author of 'Comin' thro' the Rye.' HONEY. *Fourth Edition. Crown 8vo. 6s.*

'Racy, pointed, and entertaining.'—*Vanity Fair.*
'Honey is a splendid girl.' — *Daily Express.*
'A vigorously written story, full of clever things, a piquant blend of sweet and sharp.' *Daily Telegraph.*

J. W. Mayall. THE CYNIC AND THE SYREN. *Crown 8vo. 6s.*

L. T. Meade. DRIFT. *Crown 8vo. 6s.*

Bertram Mitford. THE SIGN OF THE SPIDER. Illustrated. *Fifth Edition. Crown 8vo. 3s. 6d.*

Allan Monkhouse. LOVE IN A LIFE. *Crown 8vo. 6s.*

F. F. Montresor, Author of 'Into the Highways and Hedges.' THE ALIEN. *Second Edition. Crown 8vo. 6s.*
'Fresh, unconventional, and instinct with human sympathy.'—*Manchester Guardian.*
'Miss Montresor creates her tragedy out of passions and necessities elementarily human. Perfect art.'—*Spectator.*

Arthur Moore. THE KNIGHT PUNCTILIOUS. *Crown 8vo. 6s.*

Arthur Morrison. See page 30.

W. E. Norris. THE CREDIT OF THE COUNTY. Illustrated. *Second Edition. Crown 8vo. 6s.*
'A capital novel it is, deftly woven together of the comedy and tragedy of life.'—*Yorkshire Post.*
'It is excellent—keen, graceful, diverting.'—*Times.*
THE EMBARRASSING ORPHAN. *Crown 8vo. 6s.*
HIS GRACE. *Third Edition. Crown 8vo. 6s.*
THE DESPOTIC LADY. *Crown 8vo. 6s.*
CLARISSA FURIOSA. *Crown 8vo. 6s.*
GILES INGILBY. *Illustrated. Second Edition. Crown 8vo. 6s.*
AN OCTAVE. *Second Edition. Crown 8vo. 6s.*
A DEPLORABLE AFFAIR. *Crown 8vo. 3s. 6d.*
JACK'S FATHER. *Crown 8vo. 2s. 6d.*
LORD LEONARD THE LUCKLESS. *Crown 8vo. 6s.*
See also Fleur de Lis Novels.

Mrs. Oliphant. THE TWO MARYS. *Crown 8vo. 6s.*
THE LADY'S WALK. *Crown 8vo. 6s.*
THE PRODIGALS. *Crown 8vo. 3s. 6d.*
See also Fleur de Lis Novels.

Alfred Ollivant. OWD BOB, THE GREY DOG OF KENMUIR. *Sixth Edition. Crown 8vo. 6s.*
'Weird, thrilling, strikingly graphic.'—*Punch.*
'We admire this book . . . It is one to read with admiration and to praise with enthusiasm.'—*Bookman.*

'It is a fine, open-air, blood-stirring book, to be enjoyed by every man and woman to whom a dog is dear.'—*Literature.*

E. Phillips Oppenheim. MASTER OF MEN. *Second Edition. Crown 8vo. 6s.*

Gilbert Parker. See page 29.

James Blythe Patton. BIJLI, THE DANCER. *Crown 8vo. 6s.*

Max Pemberton. THE FOOTSTEPS OF A THRONE. Illustrated. *Second Edition. Crown 8vo. 6s.*

'A story of pure adventure, with a sensation on every page.'—*Daily Mail.*

I CROWN THEE KING. With Illustrations by Frank Dadd and A. Forrestier. *Crown 8vo. 6s.*

'A romance of high adventure, of love and war.'—*Daily News.*

Mrs. F. E. Penny. A FOREST OFFICER. *Crown 8vo. 6s.*

A MIXED MARRIAGE. *Crown 8vo. 6s.*

Eden Phillpotts. See page 30.

'Q,' Author of 'Dead Man's Rock.' THE WHITE WOLF. *Second Edition. Crown 8vo. 6s.*

'Every story is an accomplished romance in its own way.'—*Scotsman.*

'The poet's vein, the breadth of vision, the touch of mysticism are plain in all.'—*Times.*

R. Orton Prowse. THE POISON OF ASPS. *Crown 8vo. 3s. 6d.*

Richard Pryce. TIME AND THE WOMAN. *Crown 8vo. 6s.*

THE QUIET MRS. FLEMING. *Crown 8vo. 3s. 6d.*

J. Randal. AUNT BETHIA'S BUTTON. *Crown 8vo. 6s.*

Walter Raymond, Author of 'Love and Quiet Life.' FORTUNE'S DARLING. *Crown 8vo. 6s.*

Grace Rhys. THE WOOING OF SHEILA. *Second Edition. Crown 8vo. 6s.*

'A really fine book. A book that deserves to live. Sheila is the sweetest heroine who has lived in a novelist's pages for many a day. Every scene and every incident has the impress of truth. It is a masterly romance, and one that should be widely read and appreciated.'—*Morning Leader.*

Grace Rhys and Another. THE DIVERTED VILLAGE. With Illustrations by DOROTHY GWYN JEFFRIES. *Crown 8vo. 6s.*

Edith Rickert. OUT OF THE CYPRESS SWAMP. *Crown 8vo. 6s.*

W. Pett Ridge. LOST PROPERTY. *Second Edition. Crown 8vo. 6s.*

'The story is an interesting and animated picture of the struggle for life in London, with a natural humour and tenderness of its own.'—*Scotsman.*

'A simple, delicate bit of work, which will give pleasure to many. Much study of

the masses has made him, not mad, but strong, and—wonder of wonders—cheerful.' —*Times.*

A SON OF THE STATE. *Crown 8vo. 3s. 6d.*

SECRETARY TO BAYNE, M.P. *Crown 8vo. 6s.*

C. G. D. Roberts. THE HEART OF THE ANCIENT WOOD. *Crown 8vo. 3s. 6d.*

Mrs. M. H. Roberton. A GALLANT QUAKER. Illustrated. *Crown 8vo. 6s.*

W. Clark Russell. MY DANISH SWEETHEART. Illustrated. *Fourth Edition. Crown 8vo. 6s.*

W. Satchell. THE LAND OF THE LOST. *Crown 8vo. 6s.*

Marshall Saunders. ROSE A CHARLITTE. *Crown 8vo. 6s.*

W. C. Scully. THE WHITE HECATOMB. *Crown 8vo. 6s.*

BETWEEN SUN AND SAND. *Crown 8vo. 6s.*

A VENDETTA OF THE DESERT. *Crown 8vo. 6s.*

Adeline Sergeant. Author of 'The Story of a Penitent Soul.' A GREAT LADY. *Crown 8vo. 6s.*

THE MASTER OF BEECHWOOD. *Crown 8vo. 6s.*

BARBARA'S MONEY. *Second Edition. Crown 8vo. 6s.*

'Full of life and incident, and Barbara is a delightful heroine.'—*Daily Express.*

'An unusually entertaining story.'— *World.*

ANTHEA'S WAY. *Crown 8vo. 6s.*

W. F. Shannon. THE MESS DECK. *Crown 8vo. 3s. 6d.*

JIM TWELVES. *Second Edition. Crown 8vo. 3s. 6d.*

'Full of quaint humour, wise saws, and deep-sea philosophy.'—*Morning Leader.*

'In "Jim Twelves" Mr. Shannon has created a delightful character.'—*Punch.*

'Bright and lively reading throughout.'— *Telegraph.*

Helen Shipton. THE STRONG GOD CIRCUMSTANCE. *Crown 8vo. 6s.*

R. N. Stephens. A GENTLEMAN PLAYER. *Crown 8vo. 6s.*

See also Fleur de Lis Novels.

E. H. Strain. ELMSLIE'S DRAG-NET. *Crown 8vo. 6s.*

Esmé Stuart. A WOMAN OF FORTY. *Crown 8vo. 6s.*

CHRISTALLA. *Crown 8vo. 6s.*

Duchess of Sutherland. ONE HOUR AND THE NEXT. *Third Edition. Crown 8vo. 6s.*

Annie Swan. LOVE GROWN COLD. *Second Edition. Crown 8vo. 5s.*

Benjamin Swift. SIREN CITY. *Crown 8vo. 6s.*

SORDON. *Crown 8vo. 6s.*

R. B. Townshend. LONE PINE: A Romance of Mexican Life. *Crown 8vo. 6s.*

Mrs. E. W. Trafford-Taunton. SILENT DOMINION. *Crown 8vo, 6s.*

Paul Waineman. A HEROINE FROM FINLAND. *Crown 8vo. 6s.*
 'A lovely tale.'—*Manchester Guardian.*
 'A vivid picture of pastoral life in a beautiful and too little known country.'
 —*Pall Mall Gazette.*
BY A FINNISH LAKE. *Crown 8vo. 6s.*

Victor Waite. CROSS TRAILS. *Crown 8vo. 6s.*

H. B. Marriott Watson. THE SKIRTS OF HAPPY CHANCE. Illustrated. *Second Edition. Crown 8vo. 6s.*

H. G. Wells. THE STOLEN BACILLUS, and other Stories. *Second Edition. Crown 8vo. 3s. 6d.*
THE PLATTNER STORY AND OTHERS. *Second Edition. Crown 8vo. 3s. 6d.*
THE SEA LADY. *Crown 8vo. 6s.*
 'A strange, fantastic tale, a really beautiful idyll.'—*Standard.*
 'In literary charm, in inventiveness, in fun and humour, it is equal to the best of Mr. Wells' stories.'—*Daily News.*
 'Highly successful farce and plenty of polished satire.'—*Daily Mail.*
TALES OF SPACE AND TIME. *Crown 8vo. 6s.*

WHEN THE SLEEPER WAKES. *Crown 8vo. 6s.*
THE INVISIBLE MAN. *Crown 8vo. 6s.*
LOVE AND MR. LEWISHAM. *Crown 8vo. 6s.*

Stanley Weyman, Author of 'A Gentleman of France.' UNDER THE RED ROBE. With Illustrations by R. C. WOODVILLE. *Seventeenth Edition. Crown 8vo. 6s.*
 'Every one who reads books at all must read this thrilling romance, from the first page of which to the last the breathless reader is haled along. An inspiration of manliness and courage.'—*Daily Chronicle.*

Mrs. C. N. Williamson, Author of 'The Barnstormers.' PAPA. *Second Edition. Crown 8vo. 6s.*
 'Full of startling adventures and sensational episodes.'—*Daily Graphic.*
THE ADVENTURE OF PRINCESS SLYVIA. *Crown 8vo. 3s. 6d.*

C. N. and A. M. Williamson. THE LIGHTNING CONDUCTOR: Being the Romance of a Motor Car. Illustrated. *Crown 8vo. 6s.*
 'A very ingenious and diverting book.'—*Morning Leader.*

Zack, Author of 'Life is Life.' TALES OF DUNSTABLE WEIR. *Crown 8vo. 6s.*

X.L. AUT DIABOLUS AUT NIHIL. *Crown 8vo. 3s. 6d.*

The Fleur de Lis Novels

Crown 8vo. 3s. 6d.

MESSRS. METHUEN are now publishing a cheaper issue of some of their popular Novels in a new and most charming style of binding.

Andrew Balfour.
TO ARMS!

Jane Barlow.
A CREEL OF IRISH STORIES.

E. F. Benson.
THE VINTAGE.

J. Bloundelle-Burton.
IN THE DAY OF ADVERSITY.

Mrs. Caffyn (Iota).
ANNE MAULEVERER.

Mrs. W. K. Clifford.
A FLASH OF SUMMER.

L. Cope Cornford.
SONS OF ADVERSITY.

A. J. Dawson.
DANIEL WHYTE.

Menie Muriel Dowie.
THE CROOK OF THE BOUGH.

Mrs. Dudeney.
THE THIRD FLOOR.

Sara Jeannette Duncan.
A VOYAGE OF CONSOLATION.

G. Manville Fenn.
THE STAR GAZERS.

Jane H. Findlater.
RACHEL.

Jane H. and Mary Findlater.
TALES THAT ARE TOLD.

J. S. Fletcher.
THE PATHS OF THE PRUDENT.

Mary Gaunt.
KIRKHAM'S FIND.

Robert Hichens.
BYEWAYS.

Emily Lawless.
HURRISH.
MAELCHO.

W. E. Norris.
MATTHEW AUSTIN.

Mrs. Oliphant.
SIR ROBERT'S FORTUNE.

Mary A. Owen.
THE DAUGHTER OF ALOUETTE.

Mary L. Pendered.
AN ENGLISHMAN.

Morley Roberts.
THE PLUNDERERS.

R. N. Stephens.
AN ENEMY TO THE KING.

Mrs. Walford.
SUCCESSORS TO THE TITLE.

Percy White.
A PASSIONATE PILGRIM.

Books for Boys and Girls

Crown 8vo. 3s. 6d.

THE ICELANDER'S SWORD. By S. Baring-Gould.
TWO LITTLE CHILDREN AND CHING. By Edith E. Cuthell.
TODDLEBEN'S HERO. By M. M. Blake.
ONLY A GUARD-ROOM DOG. By Edith E. Cuthell.
THE DOCTOR OF THE JULIET. By Harry Collingwood.
MASTER ROCKAFELLAR'S VOYAGE. By W. Clark Russell.

SYD BELTON : Or, the Boy who would not go to Sea. By G. Manville Fenn.
THE RED GRANGE. By Mrs. Molesworth.
THE SECRET OF MADAME DE MONLUC. By the Author of 'Mdle. Mori.'
DUMPS. By Mrs. Parr.
A GIRL OF THE PEOPLE. By L. T. Meade.
HEPSY GIPSY. By L. T. Meade. 2s. 6d.
THE HONOURABLE MISS. By L. T. Meade.

The Novelist

MESSRS. METHUEN are issuing under the above general title a Monthly Series of Novels by popular authors at the price of Sixpence. Each number is as long as the average Six Shilling Novel. The first numbers of 'THE NOVELIST' are as follows :—

I. DEAD MEN TELL NO TALES. By E. W. Hornung.
II. JENNIE BAXTER, JOURNALIST. By Robert Barr.
III. THE INCA'S TREASURE. By Ernest Glanville.
IV. A SON OF THE STATE. By W. Pett Ridge.
V. FURZE BLOOM. By S. Baring-Gould.
VI. BUNTER'S CRUISE. By C. Gleig.
VII. THE GAY DECEIVERS. By Arthur Moore.
VIII. PRISONERS OF WAR. By A. Boyson Weekes.
IX. A FLASH OF SUMMER. By Mrs. W. K. Clifford.
X. VELDT AND LAAGER: Tales of the Transvaal. By E. S. Valentine.
XI. THE NIGGER KNIGHTS. By F. Norreys Connel.
XII. A MARRIAGE AT SEA. By W. Clark Russell.
XIII. THE POMP OF THE LAVILETTES. By Gilbert Parker.
XIV. A MAN OF MARK. By Anthony Hope.
XV. THE CARISSIMA. By Lucas Malet.
XVI. THE LADY'S WALK. By Mrs. Oliphant.
XVII. DERRICK VAUGHAN. By Edna Lyall..
XVIII. IN THE MIDST OF ALARMS. By Robert Barr.
XIX. HIS GRACE. By W. E. Norris.
XX. DODO. By E. F. Benson.
XXI. CHEAP JACK ZITA. By S. Baring-Gould.
XXII. WHEN VALMOND CAME TO PONTIAC. By Gilbert Parker.

XXIII. THE HUMAN BOY. By Eden Phillpotts.
XXIV. THE CHRONICLES OF COUNT ANTONIO. By Anthony Hope.
XXV. BY STROKE OF SWORD. By Andrew Balfour.
XXVI. KITTY ALONE. By S. Baring-Gould.
XXVII. GILES INGILBY. By W. E. Norris.
XXVIII. URITH. By S. Baring-Gould.
XXIX. THE TOWN TRAVELLER. By George Gissing.
XXX. MR. SMITH. By Mrs. Walford.
XXXI. A CHANGE OF AIR. By Anthony Hope.
XXXII. THE KLOOF BRIDE. By Ernest Glanville.
XXXIII. ANGEL. By B. M. Croker.
XXXIV. A COUNSEL OF PERFECTION. By Lucas Malet.
XXXV. THE BABY'S GRANDMOTHER. By Mrs. Walford.
XXXVI. THE COUNTESS TEKLA. By Robert Barr
XXXVII. DRIFT. BY L. T. Meade.
XXXVIII. THE MASTER OF BEECHWOOD. By Adeline Sergeant.
XXXIX. CLEMENTINA. By A. E. W. Mason.
XL. THE ALIEN. By F. F. Montresor.
XLI. THE BROOM SQUIRE. By S. Baring-Gould.
XLII. HONEY. By Helen Mathers.
XLIII. THE FOOTSTEPS OF A THRONE. By Max Pemberton.

Methuen's Sixpenny Library

THE MATABELE CAMPAIGN. By Major-General Baden-Powell.
THE DOWNFALL OF PREMPEH. By Major-General Baden-Powell.
MY DANISH SWEETHEART. By W. Clark Russell.
IN THE ROAR OF THE SEA. By S. Baring-Gould.
PEGGY OF THE BARTONS. By B. M. Croker.
THE GREEN GRAVES OF BALGOWRIE. By Jane H. Findlater.
THE STOLEN BACILLUS. By H. G. Wells.
MATTHEW AUSTIN. By W. E. Norris.
THE CONQUEST OF LONDON. By Dorothea Gerard.
A VOYAGE OF CONSOLATION. By Sara J. Duncan.
THE MUTABLE MANY. By Robert Barr.
BEN HUR. By General Lew Wallace.
SIR ROBERT'S FORTUNE. By Mrs. Oliphant.
THE FAIR GOD. By General Lew Wallace.
CLARISSA FURIOSA. By W. E. Norris.
CRANFORD. By Mrs. Gaskell.
NOEMI. By S. Baring-Gould.
THE THRONE OF DAVID. By J. H. Ingraham.

ACROSS THE SALT SEAS. By J. Bloundelle Burton.
THE MILL ON THE FLOSS. By George Eliot.
PETER SIMPLE. By Captain Marryat.
MARY BARTON. By Mrs. Gaskell.
PRIDE AND PREJUDICE. By Jane Austen.
NORTH AND SOUTH. By Mrs. Gaskell.
JACOB FAITHFUL. By Captain Marryat.
SHIRLEY. By Charlotte Brontë.
FAIRY TALES RE-TOLD. By S. Baring Gould.
THE TRUE HISTORY OF JOSHUA DAVIDSON. By Mrs. Lynn Linton.
A STATE SECRET. By B. M. Croker.
SAM'S SWEETHEART. By Helen Mathers.
HANDLEY CROSS. By R. S. Surtees.
ANNE MAULEVERER. By Mrs. Caffyn.
THE ADVENTURERS. By H. B. Marriott Watson.
DANTE'S DIVINE COMEDY. Translated by H. F. Cary.
THE CEDAR STAR. By M. E. Mann.
MASTER OF MEN. By E. P. Oppenheim.
THE TRAIL OF THE SWORD. By Gilbert Parker.